SUBSIDIA BIBLICA

15

subsidia biblica - 15

ROBERT C. HILL

Australian Catholic University

Breaking the Bread of the Word: Principles of Teaching Scripture

EDITRICE PONTIFICIO ISTITUTO BIBLICO — ROMA 1991

Previous publications of Robert C. Hill:

St John Chrysostom's Homilies on Genesis, Fathers of the Church 74 & 82, Washington: Catholic University of America Press, 1986, 1990.

Faith in Search of Understanding: An Introduction to Theology, Melbourne: Collins Dove, 1989.

Mystery of Life: A Theology of Church, Melbourne: Collins Dove, 1990.

ISBN 88-7653-596-9

EDITRICE PONTIFICIO ISTITUTO BIBLICO
Piazza della Pilotta 35 - 00187 Roma, Italia

To the members of the
Catholic Biblical Association of Australia
for their efforts to promote the
breaking of the bread of the Word

Preface

The ministry of the Word in the Christian tradition goes back to biblical times. The ideal of that ministry has been beautifully restated in our day in Vatican II's Constitution on Divine Revelation *Dei Verbum*, which speaks of the bread of life being unceasingly taken from the table of the Word, as from the table of the body of the Lord, and offered to the faithful (#21). That there have been periods between those high points when the bread of the Word was not so readily taken and broken for the faithful, owing to neglect of preparation of its ministers, is the reason for this volume. Hopefully, more deliberate attention to the ministry of the Word, especially by its teachers and those who form them, will promote the realisation of that beautiful ideal.

My own formal introduction to the text of the Word was enhanced by periods of study at the Pontifical Biblical Institute, which since its foundation in 1909 by Pope Pius X with his letter *Vinea Electa* has been preparing ministers of the Word for his 'chosen vineyard'. During these periods of study at the Biblicum, firstly during the Council and then two decades later, I raised with its directors the question of attention to principles of ministry in addition to textual and contextual study in biblical formation, and was encouraged by them to work on a project for such a curriculum for biblical institutes through composition of a text dealing with these principles. Experience in the meantime in biblical education, teacher preparation and adult education has reinforced my conviction of the need for such attention to ministry in general and the particular ministry of teaching the Scriptures.

A text, of course, is limited in its impact; only if it influences the preparation of ministers, especially through adjustments to institutional curricula and the continuing formation of those already in service, will it meet the need. In itself, though, this text has benefited from the experience and advice of specialists: from James Swetnam SJ, vice-rector of the Biblicum, and from two of my colleagues at ACU, Jude Butcher CFC, former Head of Education, and Marcellin Flynn FMS, author of works on religious education. These mentors have generously read successive drafts of this work and commented on them from their particular expertise, and I am indebted to them. As well, without Michael Bezzina's ready assistance, this text could never have been prepared for printing; thank you, Michael.

I have been conscious in the composition of this text of my unfamiliarity with practices and literature of other languages and cultures than my own, and yet the ministry of the Word (and a text on it) needs to take account of these, as I am at pains to stress. I hope that in outlining general principles I am not presuming or conflicting too greatly in my ignorance of other cultural situations.

Hopefully, these limitations notwithstanding, this text will promote that ideal of breaking the bread of the Word by adequately prepared ministers.

Robert C. Hill,
Australian Catholic University,
Sydney

Table of Contents

Part One: The Ministry of the Word

Part One

The ministry of the Word

Introduction

This book is about helping people come to an appreciation of the gift of the Word of God. Quite some years ago (though still within living memory), I encountered an elderly Religious, teacher of twelve year-olds, in my work as roving religious education consultant. Having been raised in a different Church in preconciliar times, he was venting his exasperation at the school's choice of texts that year for his class in 'Christian Doctrine': "We don't have a book with doctrine in it this time," he fumed; "we've only got the New Testament." Amusing though it was to me as a student of the Word, his reply said much of the model of Church in which he was raised, its priorities in terms of forms of tradition, its preparation of its ministers, the consequent degree of appreciation by Catholic people and Catholic teachers of the role of the Word in their life and ministry.

Today, happily, greater numbers of the Catholic faithful are sensing both the need they have to meet the Word of God in the Scriptures and the deprivation that the Catholic community, by comparison with some other Christian communities, has previously suffered in this regard. Many factors have contributed to this overdue recognition of the place of the scriptural Word in Christian life. Much is now being done to make the ideal of a life that is both scriptural and eucharistic a reality for Catholics everywhere. The contention of this book is that the ministry of the Word, and in particular the teaching of the Scriptures, is still **a neglected area in Catholic formation**, whatever of the growing esteem for the Scriptures themselves; and that such neglect can be remedied.

Perhaps that seems a sweeping as well as a negative generalisation, considering for one thing the amount of attention to the ministry of the Word in magisterial statement at least since *Providentissimus Deus* in 1893, as Chapter One itself outlines. To establish its truth empirically one would need to gauge the benefits Catholics generally are experiencing at the hands of those ministers; the author's or the reader's own experience does not, of course, suffice. In the face of the impossibility of such a comprehensive survey, two simpler measures are suggested: look at **the amount of writing on the ministry of the Word** by Catholics in any language, and inspect **the curricula of Catholic institutes** preparing people for that ministry. On both scores one would have to admit that the challenge to bring the faithful to meet the Word of God has not been wholeheartedly accepted.

1. Developed understanding of Church

At least we have come to acknowledge the importance of the scriptural Word for us, owing to several developmental factors. We have come to understand the Church more profoundly: Bellarmine's societal model that dominated Catholic ecclesiology and life for centuries after the Reformation no longer suffices. We have been led from one biblical figure, the Church as body of Christ, presented to us by Pope Pius XII earlier this century, to the less static, more dynamic figure of the People of God, a community on the move towards fulfilment, nourished by the scriptural Word and the eucharistic banquet - the ideal of Vatican II. We have proceeded beyond the figures and images **to see Church as mystery and communion**, a divine plan that offers us life; Vatican II and the 1985 and 1987 Synods highlighted these themes. Knowledge of the Scriptures has contributed to this development and in turn has been promoted by appreciation of the role of the Word in this unfolding mystery: ideally - but not yet in fact - the People on the march should be constantly pondering the pattern of God's action on their behalf that the Bible offers them. Movement and change are characteristic of such a community, and growth in the knowledge of God's Word is part of this eschatological movement. The sharing, participation, fellowship that distinguish **the model of Church as communion**, *koinonia*, urge us to accept fully the offer of life and light given us by God in the Scriptures.

Catholic scholars have come to feel more at home with the Bible as their appreciation of biblical models of Church has grown. If they were not encouraged to be in the vanguard of biblical research in the centuries following the Reformation, it was because in the ecclesiastical society of those times the deposit of faith was seen more as a package to be faithfully transmitted from one generation to the next, not unpacked for an investigation of its riches; the Old Testament, Paul and the author of *Hebrews* could be invoked for encouragement of this kind of uncritical fidelity in traditional processes. Societal models of community do not promote the activity of investigative thinkers and researchers pushing ahead of official policy. Only tentatively, in the wake of *Providentissimus Deus*, and even less adventurously after *Lamentabili* and *Pascendi* in 1907, did Catholic scholars enter the field of biblical criticism to which their Oratorian colleague Richard Simon had beckoned them in the seventeenth century.

2. Advances in biblical science

Discoveries had been made by archeologists and other researchers in the intervening centuries that had richly resourced the branches of 'lower criticism': there was greater confidence in the accuracy of biblical texts due to the discovery of more and more manuscripts, knowledge of the biblical languages to take advantage of these texts was similarly made more precise, so that the process of exegesis became more fruitful. To this process 'higher criticism' offered further skills. Literary criticism enabled exegetes to study the sources available to the sacred authors and the purposes they had in mind in employing them as well as the freedom with which they selected, reshaped and explained the material coming to them from an earlier period of transmission, perhaps in oral form. Form critics were interested particularly in the shapes and forms and genres in which traditional material had been transmitted and how these forms appeared in the biblical texts now in our hands. As well, we came to know more about the world and the particular societies in which the biblical authors lived, as well as the contemporary literatures that existed beyond the sacred canon. In short, **biblical scholars could appreciate more fully** the way the Word of God was incarnated in the language and literature of the Bible, and so could approach it in a manner analogous to that of students of other bodies of literature. The package could be unwrapped to glimpse its riches for our benefit without impairing the fidelity of its transmission to succeeding generations.

These possibilities became, after that initial hesitancy, a reality for Catholic biblical scholarship from the midpoint of the twentieth century with Pius XII's charter for biblical studies, *Divino Afflante Spiritu* in 1943, the Pontifical Biblical Commission's adopting a positive attitude to New Testament scholarship in its 1964 Instruction on the historical truth of the Gospels, *Sancta Mater Ecclesia*, and Vatican II's Constitution on Divine Revelation, *Dei Verbum*, in 1965. Catholic scholars could now make the most of all those skills and resources developed by the more biblical communities, and they have generally embraced the opportunity. "Roman Catholic scholarship" is no longer synonymous with outdated conservatism; the Catholic community is no longer suspicious of the Bible at the official level.

3. Gap between knowledge and communication

As the magisterium has continued to remind scholars, however, "the sacred Books were not given by God to satisfy people's curiosity or to provide them with an object of study and research" (*DAS*). **The very notion of *koinonia* that characterises the divine offer of life in both Church and Scriptures demands a communication of that life**; the Scriptures themselves insist on it. Which brings us back to our regrettable opening thesis and its indices: the ministry of the Word to the faithful, and in particular the preparation of the ministers, is still a neglected area, to the great detriment of Christian life; suffice it to look at available Catholic literature and the curriculum of Catholic institutes of biblical learning. Whatever of the current level of Catholic biblical scholarship, its fruits are not reaching the Catholic community generally, and a principal reason for this is that we are not making scholars apostles.

If Vatican II's ideal of a Christian life that is both eucharistic and scriptural is to become a reality, this serious situation must be corrected. Too long have we expected people to draw their nourishment from the table of the body of the Lord and not also from the table of the Word of God. In my work of preparing Catholic graduate teachers for the task of religious education I usually ask them this question: how scriptural was your home / your schooling / your parish / your initial professional formation / your teaching / your later professional formation? Rarely do I encounter one of these Catholic adults who does not have to admit that only at the latter end of the spectrum does any substantial scriptural colouring occur (as I have to admit it myself). Further, in my experience of higher institutes of biblical learning over several decades, I have yet to find amongst a range of excellent courses on textual and contextual study of the Bible **a substantial component of the curriculum** designed to prepare these budding scholars (mostly priests) specifically for the ministry of the Word in its various forms, beyond personal study of the sacred text.

When I have asked those responsible for the curriculum in these institutions - generally excellent scholars - the reason why nothing is done to set out for future teachers of the Bible the principles of teaching and to provide some learning experiences, the answer has generally been as follows (to quote one): "Our concern is to prepare our students to understand the biblical text... Communication of the biblical message is not the direct concern of this Institute." In this stance there is something of clinical professionalism, an unwillingness to venture beyond one's own area of expertise. But that simply perpetuates the problem; it is obviously **false to the principle of incarnation** to expect these young scholars to acquire the skill of teaching by osmosis or inspiration instead of through the normal processes of instruction and practice. Working on that supposition leads predictably to students modelling later teaching on their mentors' own style in higher education which, even if not necessarily less than exemplary from a pedagogical point of view, creates problems in a quite different context; microscopic exegesis is not good ministry to the parish Bible group. The result has been the release onto the Catholic faithful of graduates entrusted with Christian formation who have **basic deficiencies as communicators**, with the consequences we have outlined.

4. Preparation for ministry

What, precisely, is required in the formation of a minister of the Word? There should, firstly, be some general attention to the scriptural Word and to ministry, to recognising that the Word was spoken to take effect, to be communicated. This arises in the context of the study of revelation as *koinonia*, divine self-communication; leaving people with a theology of revelation as that unwrapped package will undermine effective ministry. The relationship between Word and ministry needs to be looked at; the bread of the Word is to be broken, as biblical commentators from patristic preachers onwards have prided themselves on doing and the magisterium has reinforced, at least this century. And if we are to affect the curriculum of biblical institutes, we must challenge that premise that study of the Word suffices without consideration of ministry. That should provide a sound platform, and constitutes the subject matter of **Chapter One** here.

As basic and as urgent is consideration of the condition of the recipient of the Word, the beneficiary of ministry, those for whom the bread is broken - their needs, their abilities and gifts, their age and sex, their general readiness for the Word; treating children as adults, and adults as children, is something preachers and teachers have been guilty of in the past. The ministry of the Word has much to learn from human sciences that have studied human development and ways of learning - cognitive and moral development, development in faith and religion: why should these findings not be utilised to assist the Word? A basic principle of ministry is fidelity to the biblical message and fidelity to the condition of the learner; **Chapter Two** deals with this principle.

A particular application of this incarnational principle of double fidelity in the ministry of the Word may be termed inculturation. The biblical Word, like the Jesus of history, comes to us with a cultural conditioning of its own that affects its receptivity by modern readers/listeners in the West; they themselves are conditioned by their own culture which affects their response to the Word. Ministers of the Word need to acknowledge the cultural conditioning on both sides and the way teaching and learning are affected by the attitudes, experience, technology, social patterns of the learners. Paul's different approaches to Jewish and Gentile audiences may serve as a model here (**Chapter Three**).

A fourth consideration for good ministry is the form it takes and the context where it occurs. Vatican II may be able to speak traditionally of "pastoral preaching, catechesis and all Christian instruction", but we need to distinguish as well different levels and models of instruction and the contribution to ministry of the artists, the scholarly commentators, the Bible translators. We need to acknowledge also the impact of changes in society on traditional contexts of ministry: the decline of the parish as a basic unit in favour of neighbourhood, workplace, club, the decline of 'hot' media like the printed word in the face of competition from 'cool' media like movie and television, the decline of formal instructional situations like lecture halls (and large churches) in favour of more participative settings favouring interchange and involvement. Like Ezekiel visiting the exiles in Bablyon to "sit where they sat," the minister needs to appreciate the situation of today's communities and adjust accordingly - this is the message of **Chapter Four**.

It is not enough to prepare ministers of the Word for their task by raising a series of general issues like the above; they must also plan carefully for the exercise of their particular ministry if the Word is to take effect. Such planning for ministry begins with broad aims and goals: am I clear precisely why I am preaching to this congregation, working with this class of children, this group of adults, this prayer group? Am I bringing the Word to them because they need it right now, because the Church is in favour of biblical instruction, because people should have a sound biblical culture, because these children must meet Jesus in the Scriptures, because these students need to see the whole pattern of the mystery of Christ? Beyond being clear about rationale, I need also plan carefully about the knowledge and understandings, skills, attitudes and values that I can impart in this session with this group: can I launch straight into Isaian theology, or do my listeners still need help to locate Isaiah in the Bible? Successful planning for ministry is about rationale, objectives, strategies, outcomes, as educationists have shown in various ministries (**Chapter Five**).

5. Purpose of a text such as this

Such considerations need to be built into a curriculum designed to prepare ministers of the Word for whatever kind of involvement with others, in addition of course to equally professional study of the sacred text. For would-be teachers of Scripture there are additional considerations, that occur here in Part II. Ideally, there should be other texts devoted to the other ministries as well, but my expertise does not lie in that direction. If this text remains a text and does not influence the shape of curriculum in places where ministers of the Word are being formed, it will have failed in its purpose: no one ever learnt to be a teacher through reading a book alone. It is being written only with the concession that in some situations **curriculum development requires such a text** as a blueprint. It is also being written out of a conviction that a desperate situation of neglect can be remedied by quite obvious, well-tried procedures. If the same sense of urgency and frustration evidenced in these opening pages does not pervade the whole text, it is in the belief that spleen does not make as good exposition as serenity and clarity.

May our ministers of the Word, and our Scripture teachers in particular, receive the kind of preparation this vital ministry demands, for the benefit of the faithful longing to enter into the "*koinonia* with the Father and his Son Jesus Christ" (1 Jn 1.3) that the Scriptures make possible and themselves represent.

Chapter One

Word and Ministry

Outline

Preparation for ministry of the Word is determined by several basic considerations of the Word of God itself and the need to communicate it:

- the Word has been spoken, and is intended to take effect, not lie dormant;

- the Word comes in the context of God's sharing of life, *koinonia*, in both the historical and the scriptural incarnation;

- the bread of life that is the scriptural Word needs to be broken for the faithful, who have for too long been deprived of that ministry, despite recent encouragement from the magisterium;

- study of the sacred text is directed towards effective communication; both require particular skills.

1. A Word to be communicated

The reverence of believers for the Sacred Scriptures is primarily reverence for a Word, the Word of God. Study of the text we hold sacred also rests on this more basic truth. The Creed of 381 that we know as Nicene refers to the scriptural Word in these same terms: "He has spoken through the prophets (*per prophetas*, διὰ τῶν προφητῶν)," where the accent falls on the Word first spoken and then relayed through the "prophets" in the sense of the biblical composers. For the Fathers of that Council, the Scriptures are best related to **the spoken Word of God**; and our most recent Council, with patristic encouragement, deliberately insists on that relationship between text and Word in a Constitution entitled, significantly, *Dei Verbum*.

The biblical composers themselves are in no doubt that it is God's word that they are relaying, that "this is the Word of the Lord." They are equally certain that this is not a word spoken idly, that **the word is spoken to take effect.** The prophetic and historical literature of the Old Testament, the Nebi'im of the Hebrew Bible, in particular rested firmly on this principle that "the word of our God will stand forever" (Is 40.8 - a most appropriate motto for Rome's Pontifical Biblical Institute, commissioned as it is to prepare people to bring the Word of God to its intended recipients). Isaiah had more to say on the subject:

> For as the rain and the snow come down from heaven,
> and return not thither but water the earth,
> making it bring forth and sprout,
> giving seed to the sower and bread to the eater,
> so shall my word that goes forth from my mouth;
> it shall not return to me empty,
> but it shall accomplish that which I purpose,
> and prosper in the thing for which I sent it (55.10-11).

Preachers and composers working in the light of the Incarnation of the Word and his Paschal Mystery enjoyed clearer insight into the purpose of this Word and **the effect intended for human beneficiaries.** For Paul "it is the power of God for salvation to everyone who has faith," and the way to faith for us all is the proclamation of this Word (Rom 1.16; 10.14-17). For the author of the Pastoral Epistles the inspired scriptural Word "is profitable for teaching, for reproof, for correction, and for training in righteousness" (2 Tim 3.16). These preachers and composers see themselves engaged in this ministry of the Word to the audience envisaged by him who has spoken.

Patristic commentators and later theologians were thus in a position to reflect on the saving purpose of the scriptural Word in relation to the historical Incarnation. For John Chrysostom, for example, both alike exemplify **that wonderful divine considerateness,** *synkatabasis,* demonstrated in acceptance of human limitations for the sake of our salvation. In his commentary on *Genesis* Chrysostom moves from one incarnation to the other:

> He had constantly in mind the welfare of human beings, providing inspired authors and through them performing signs and wonders.... God, as though taking pity on our race, sent us a healer of our souls and bodies by plucking his only-begotten Son from the Father's bosom, as it were, to take the form of a slave and be born of a virgin, to spend his life with us and endure all our limitations so as to lift our human nature lying under all its sins and raise it from earth to heaven. No wonder the Son of Thunder is amazed and cried aloud as he sees the extent of God's love shown to the human race, 'God so loved the world.'[1]

Small wonder that the recent magisterium acknowledges Chrysostom in documenting **the saving purpose of the Word,** as Pope Pius XII does in *Divino Afflante Spiritu* [2] and Vatican II in that carefully articulated comparison of the two incarnations in *Dei Verbum* that follows Chrysostom's theology of the Word.[3]

So the Word of God in the Scriptures is a Word to be communicated, a Word meant to take effect in the welfare of the listener. With that purpose in view **the scriptural text serves the spoken Word,** it does not imprison it. We may find an analogy in the sound of music: the beauty of the composer's notes, originating with him, is shared by the listeners as he performs his piece; musical notation can register the notes for posterity, but only a further performance by musicians will bring the notes to life again and produce the effect intended in other listeners. So Paul can say, "Faith comes from what is heard... and how are they to hear without a preacher?" Between the Word and the faith of believers occurs the ministry of the Word in the person of teachers, preachers, catechists and other ministers. We recall Clement's story of the way Mark's Gospel came to be, in the account of Eusebius:

> After Peter had publicly proclaimed the Word in Rome and by the Spirit had preached the Gospel, the considerable audience

---

[1] Homily 27 on *Genesis* (*PG* 53,240).
[2] *AAS* 35 (1943) 297-326.
[3] *Dei Verbum* 13.

besought Mark to write the words down, as a man who had
followed him for a long time and remembered what had been
said. He did so, and made his Gospel available to those who
asked for it. When Peter got to know of this, he neither took
strong exception to it nor did he encourage it. [4]

For Peter the Gospel exists primarily in its oral communication to
the listeners, whereas **a text is derivative and secondary**. The
Word is to be communicated as directly as possible.

2. Revelation as *koinonia*

Significantly, Vatican II's Constitution *Dei Verbum* on
divine revelation begins with the opening verses of the first
epistle of John, where the theme is the communication of life,
koinonia; for that is what revelation basically is for the Council,
divine self-communication. The author of the epistle insists that
his message of life is not some abstract treatment of the topic: he
has met Life personally, heard his voice, touched him, in the
person of the Incarnate Word, and so he is well qualified to speak
of the Word of life to others. And not simply speak: the share in
life that the Father has accorded him in the Word he can share
with his community by **a sharing of the Word**, *koinonia.* God
communicates to us his life through the Word.

> That which was from the beginning, which we have heard,
> which we have seen with our eyes,
> which we have looked upon and touched with our hands,
> concerning the Word of life -
> the life was made manifest, and we saw it, and testify to it,
> and proclaim to you the eternal life
> which was with the Father and was made manifest to us -
> that which we have seen and heard we proclaim also to you,
> so that you may have *koinonia* with us;
> and our *koinonia* is with the Father and with his son Jesus Christ.
> We are writing this that our joy may be complete (1 Jn 1.1-4).

---

[4] *Historia Ecclesiastica* 6,14,6-7 (SC 41,107).

It is a beautifully personal theology of revelation that the Council has thus chosen, well bringing out the saving purpose of the divine initiative, "so that by hearing the message of salvation the whole world may believe; by believing, it may hope; and by hoping, it may love" (*DV* 1), in the words of St Augustine.[5] This purpose does not always emerge from the **various models of revelation** distinguished by contemporary commentators like Dulles, who lists a propositional model, an historical model, an experiential model, a dialectical model, a consciousness model, but nowhere speaks of *koinonia* or sharing.[6] Some ministers of the Word, catechists in particular, with a concern for fidelity in transmitting the Word, speak of revelation in terms of an unwrapped package, to be handed on as received. John's message, on the other hand, is all about communication, fellowship, sharing the Word of life; and that is what the ministry of the Word is about - not basically about packages or propositions or even salvation history.

> In the fulness of time, God communicated his very self to humankind and "the Word was made flesh"... From that moment communication among human beings found its highest ideal and supreme example in God, who had become man and brother.[7]

An adequate theology of the Word, as of the ministry of the Word, will begin where Chrysostom and John began - with **the paradigm of the Incarnation**. This will enable us to see the Word and the ministry of the Word in the context of the other sacraments, something obscured in theology since the Middle Ages. The relationship was not obscure in the Fathers. Origen, great catechist that he is, presents the ideal balance:

---

[5] *De Catechizandis Rudibus* 4,8 (*PL* 40,316).

[6] A. Dulles, *Models of Revelation*.

[7] Pontifical Council for the Instruments of Social Communication, *Communio et Progressio* (Pastoral Instruction on the Means of Social Communication), *AAS* 63 (1971) 597.

> You, who are accustomed to share in the holy mysteries,
> remember how cautiously and reverently you receive the body of
> the Lord, taking care that not even the smallest particle slip to the
> floor, so that absolutely nothing of the consecrated gift be lost.
> You rightly believe yourself at fault if anything of it falls through
> your neglect. If you display such caution in the protection of his
> body, how can you believe it to be a lesser fault to treat the Word
> of God with neglect.[8]

A phrase like "Word and sacrament" may be commonly used today; but it does tend to depress the fact that **the Word acts like the other sacraments** for our salvation, and must be appreciated at that level of sensible reality communicating spiritual benefit: no magic abracadabra is at work.

That scriptural and patristic balance has now been restored (if not yet everywhere in practice) at least in the beautiful ideal set forth in *Dei Verbum*'s chapter on Sacred Scripture in the life of the Church: "The Church has always venerated the divine Scriptures just as she has the very body of the Lord, since especially in the sacred liturgy she does not cease to take **the bread of life from the table of both the Word of God and the Body of Christ**, and offer it to the faithful" (*DV* 21). That is what lends such dignity to the ministry of the Word, the fulfilment of the Johannine and patristic ideal of communication of life. As suggested above, there is some way to go before the practice of that ministry attains the ideal, particularly in the Catholic tradition.

3. A bread to be broken

That beautiful ideal of Chapter 6 of *Dei Verbum* highlights the purpose of the Scriptures and the role of the ministry of the Word. Through the Scriptures God offers the faithful the bread of life, as he does in the other sacraments; the Christian people

---

[8] Homily 13 on *Exodus* (PG 12,391).

depend equally for their spiritual nourishment on Word and (other) sacraments, and this need is met by ministers empowered to take the bread of life from the table and break it open for them. For it is a bread to be broken; **it cannot nourish otherwise**. The paradigm of the Incarnation reinforces this truth: the Word, incarnate in his earthly life as in the human condition of oral and written discourse, calls for understanding, appreciation, acceptance - something that does not happen automatically for hearers and readers, as if by magic. Hence the urgency of need for solid study of the Word and competent ministry of it to the faithful, if the bread of life is not to remain undigested.

St Augustine appreciated this **relationship between Word and ministry,** as his dictum illustrates, "Intellige ut credas, crede ut intelligas." He is dealing in Sermon 43 with the interplay and interdependence of faith and understanding, and is making the point that a true faith is an informed faith: again magic is not compatible with the Incarnation. He quotes Isaiah 7.9 in the Septuagint version, "If you do not believe, you will not understand," and the dialogue between Jesus and the father of the tormented child in Mark 9 about belief and unbelief. So he enunciates his dictum about faith and understanding; but aware that it could seem somewhat rationalistic, and yet insistent that his role as a minister of the Word is also vital, he fills it out:

> So, understand with a view to faith; have faith with a view to understanding. I will explain in a nutshell how to take this without giving rise to controversy: Understand my word with a view to faith; have faith in God's word with a view to understanding.[9]

His congregation accepts God's word in faith, while Augustine's own commentary promotes their understanding of it in a way that corrects their unbelief, as Mark's character recognises. The

---

[9] *PL* 38,258.

Word, a bread to be broken, requires the ministry of the Word if faith is to be nourished.

All the great **patristic homilists and catechists** recognised the importance of this role in view of the difficulty of the Scriptures; it was early acknowledged that even in New Testament writings "there are some things hard to understand, which the ignorant and unstable twist to their own destruction, as they do the other Scriptures" (2 Pet 3.16). Chrysostom in the East had no little esteem for the service he rendered his congregation in Antioch (and later in Constantinople). Not that he regarded them as completely untutored, because occasionally he could allow them to choose between alternative interpretations; but he knew that his commentary was essential if the scriptural text was to come alive for them - hence his exasperation with them if they let their attention wander, as on that occasion when the church lamplighter distracted them:

> Look alive now, and shake off your lethargy. Why do I say this? We are explaining the Scriptures to you, while you are turning your eyes away from us and directing them instead to the lamps and the man lighting them. Such laziness! to turn away from us and attend to him. Here am I, lighting the fire of Scripture, and the lamp of its teaching is enkindled on my lips. Its light is stronger and purer than the light you're looking at; we don't light it from a wick dipped in oil, like that one - instead, minds glowing with piety we enkindle from the ardour of their own attention.[10]

The challenge for ministers of the Word lies not simply in the fact that the Scriptures are "hard to understand" but also in the unfamiliarity and even ignorance of them by the faithful. Despite the lofty ideal enunciated today in *Dei Verbum*, the bread of life has in fact not always been taken from the table of the Word of God and offered to them. **In the Catholic tradition,**

---

[10] Sermon 4 on *Genesis* (PG 54,597).

vast numbers are simply unacquainted with the Scriptures; it can only be described as a tragedy that they are deprived of one of the principal sources of spiritual nourishment mentioned in *Dei Verbum*, and that however eucharistic their spirituality it is hardly scriptural (unlike the congregations of Augustine and Chrysostom). Nor is the Catholic community everywhere to the fore in promoting ready access to the scriptural Word, by comparison with the Bible Societies; in many countries an occasion such as Bible Sunday is still a non-event, despite the activities recently of the Catholic Biblical Federation for the biblical apostolate. Again, it could be said that it is the Catholic community that has perhaps been less well served by its ministers of the Word; homiletics has been a neglected area, inspirational preaching does not distinguish the average celebrant of the liturgy of the Word, schools and adult education institutes are not well provided with biblical programs and teachers versed in the Scriptures. Perhaps the Catholic model of Church is less consciously that of herald than is true of the Reformed traditions of Christianity. To a large extent **the bread remains to be broken**; plenty of scope yet for attention to the ministry of the Word.

4. The magisterium on the ministry of the Word

This is true despite official encouragement from the magisterium, at least over the last half century, if not for the intervening period since the Reformers' promotion of "Scriptura sola" and a predictable if regrettable Catholic knee-jerk reaction. Bellarmine's non-biblical model of Church as perfect society that prevailed in official circles **since the Counter Reformation** did not recognise the urgency of need of the faithful for frequent recourse to the Scriptures in the vernacular. And so it was all the more welcome that **Leo XIII** in 1893 should (if cautiously) recognise the need for a rejuvenated ministry of the Word in his encyclical *Providentissimus Deus* encouraging biblical study:

> We are moved and even impelled by the solicitude of the apostolic office not only to desire that this preeminent source of Catholic revelation be made available more securely and abundantly for the welfare of the Lord's flock, but also not to suffer that it be abused in any way by those who either assail Sacred Scripture by open and irreverent attack or falsely and imprudently advance certain novelties.[11]

Perhaps not a lengthy or resounding endorsement of the principle expressed later by Vatican II in so fulsome a manner; but the climate was different then, and the Pope's encouragement was reinforced in a practical manner with the establishment of the Pontifical Biblical Commission by the letter *Vigilantiae* in 1902. The climate of those years explains also his successor's guarded support for biblical study and the ministry of the Word. Concern about Modernist tendencies led to recommendation being qualified with caution in **Pius X**'s letter *Quoniam in re biblica* regarding seminary courses in Sacred Scripture:

> Biblical study has perhaps never been so important as it is today, and so it is absolutely necessary that young clerics should be assiduously trained in the knowledge of the Scriptures, so that they may not only know and understand the force and character and teaching of the Bible, but that they may be skilfully and rightly trained in the ministry of the Divine Word, and able to defend the books written by the inspiration of God against the attacks of those who deny that anything has been divinely handed down to us.[12]

Even if we in our less agitated times would express the need for this double fidelity differently, there is no doubting the Pope's insistence on the saving effect of the ministry of the Word.

Again, though contemporary anxieties about the teaching of the Bible among other things surface in the decree *Lamentabili*

---

[11] *ASS* 26 (1893-94) 270.
[12] *ASS* 39 (1906) 77.

and the encyclical *Pascendi* in 1907, two years later the Pope takes the positive step of establishing the **Pontifical Biblical Institute** in Rome with his letter *Vinea electa*.13 The Biblicum arose as an expression of the Pope's concern for the scriptural education of the whole Church: "From the very outset of our apostolic ministry we have followed in the footsteps of our predecessors in bringing every effort to bear that the chosen vineyard of Sacred Scripture might yield ever richer fruit for the pastors of the Church and for all the faithful." All the resources of the Biblicum - staff, courses, library - are meant to achieve this end; the courses in particular are to have a practical character to develop students' pedagogical skills. Modernist errors, however, are also in focus in the letter.

It took the lapse of several decades for a complete change of climate, in which the Scriptures could be seen less as problem area than as saving mystery, and the ministry of the Word as necessary concomitant of sound scriptural study. In 1943, on the fiftieth anniversary of *Providentissimus Deus*, **Pius XII** issued a wholehearted charter for biblical studies in *Divino Afflante Spiritu* urging scholars to take advantage of modern developments. At the same time the Pope recommended scholars to bring these historical, archeological, philological and other auxiliary sciences to bear on the theological import of the text so as to provide commentaries that "may help all the faithful to lead a life that is holy and worthy of a Christian," and thus cancel the complaint that biblical study is fruitless and barren.14 He holds up the example of the great patristic commentators in making his point of the saving purpose of the Word and **the need for an enthusiastic ministry of the Word:**

> The sacred books were not given by God to satisfy people's curiosity or to provide them with an object of study and research. Instead, as the Apostle observes, these divine oracles were given

---

13 *AAS* 1 (1909) 447-51.
14 *AAS* 35 (1943) 310-311.

that "they might instruct us to salvation by the faith which is in Christ Jesus," and "that the person dedicated to God might be perfect, fit for every good work."[15]

The biblical revival that followed *Divino Afflante Spiritu*, contemporary also with renewed interest in patristic studies, brought about an appreciation of the urgency of the ministry of the Word in its various forms that **chapter 6 of *Dei Verbum*** in 1965 itemises. The principle is stated there (and elsewhere in Vatican II: cf *Presbyterorum Ordinis* 18, *Perfectae Caritatis* 6) of the irreplaceable role in Christian formation of Word and Eucharist together - something familiar to the early Church but later obscured by neglect, theological imbalance and polemic. This principle is then applied to the ministry of the Word, which "includes pastoral preaching, catechesis and every type of Christian instruction, among which the liturgical homily should have pride of place." Biblical study should be pursued in such a way "that as many ministers of the divine Word as possible will be able to provide the nourishment of the Scriptures in generous measure for the people of God." A commitment is made for the Catholic community to be more active in making vernacular versions of the Scriptures available.

The ideal, of course, has yet to be achieved in its fulness. The Church's magisterium, however, has at least returned to a serene conviction of the nexus between study of the scriptural Word and ministry of that Word to the faithful. **In the years since Vatican II** the theme has been further explored in papal statements, *Evangelii Nuntiandi* (1975) of Paul VI and *Catechesi Tradendae* (1979) and *Redemptoris Missio* (1991) of John Paul II, who has himself been modelling this ministry of the Word in his weekly audiences.

---

[15] *Ibid.*, 320.

5. Scriptural study and ministry

The magisterium has endorsed the principle that we realise intuitively, of the share of the scriptural text in the saving purpose of the Word. Theologians have also explored this nexus. St Thomas, in commenting on that passage from the Pastorals we cited before (2 Tim 3.16), says: "Thus the effect of Sacred Scripture is fourfold: in the speculative order, to teach truth and refute falsehood; in the practical order, to rescue from evil and incite to good. Its ultimate effect is to lead people to perfection."[16] Protestant theologians likewise: Karl Barth speaks of a continuity between the Word of God who is God himself, the written word, and the word that is preached; Paul Tillich speaks similarly in expanding the series to six terms.[17] **This continuity and its saving implications** are no better expressed than in patristic and medieval commentators on the scriptural text itself:

> You remember that it is the one Word of God that occurs throughout all the Scriptures, that it is the one Word who is heard speaking in the many sacred writers, he who was in the beginning God with God, and so has no need of syllables because he is not affected by the restriction of time. Yet we should not be surprised that as a concession to our limitations he has deigned to take on the elements of our speech since he deigned to take on our bodily limitations.[18]

> All divine Scripture is one book, and that one book is Christ, because divine Scripture speaks of Christ and all divine Scripture is fulfilled in Christ.[19]

Study of the sacred text, as Pius XII reminded scholars, has as its end the communication of the Spirit speaking "through the

---

[16] Comm. on 2 *Tim* 3.16,17 (Turin: Marietti, 1929, 251).

[17] Quoted by A. Léonard, "Vers une théologie de la parole de Dieu" in *La Parole de Dieu en Jesus Christ*; ET "Toward a theology of the Word of God" in K. Rahner et al, *The Word. Readings in Theology*, 81-82.

[18] St Augustine, *En. in Ps CIII* (PL 37,1378).

[19] Hugh of St Victor, *De Arca Noe* (PL 176,642).

prophets"; that is the nature of the *koinonia* that is divine revelation and life, as we have seen. It is instructive to recognise both the **connection** and the **distinction** between **textual study and communication**. Failure to acknowledge the relationship would lead to the kind of barren commentary regretted by the Pope and the deprivation of a needy faithful. The analogy with musical inspiration recurs: music that remains imprisoned in notation is as anomalous and regrettable as a non-playing musician. The gift is given for others, like all charisms - or, in other words, the bread is there to be broken.

On the other hand, it is also useful to distinguish scientific study of Scripture from communication of the biblical message. As the one requires the application of certain particular skills, so does the other; both require separate development. Success in the ministry of the Word depends upon deliberate and assiduous attention to the appropriate principles and skills. The Incarnation, which offers us a paradigm for the study of the scriptural Word, also forbids our presuming that the art of communication comes to a person automatically, without effort; instruction in this highly developed field is required, introduction to a vast range of modern resources, as well as practice in employing principles, skills, techniques and resources. Today's audiences, the listening/reading/viewing public, have been encouraged to hold **high expectations of communications media;** it would be unfortunate, tragic even, if the ministry of the Word of God to his people disappointed these expectations through ignorance or lethargy on the part of the minister when, as Chrysostom would remind us, the divine author of the Scriptures has in his *synkatabasis* accommodated himself so lovingly to their human condition "for the sake of our salvation".

'God left him, ascending at the spot where he had been talking with him' (Gn 35.13). See the extent of the considerateness (*synkatabasis*) of these expressions of Sacred Scripture. 'God ascended,' it says - not to have us consider that the divinity is circumscribed in place, but that we might learn from this his unspeakable love, namely, that the grace of the Spirit shows considerateness for our human limitations and describes everything in this way. Ascending and descending, of course, are not properly applied to God; but since it is a particular token of his unspeakable love that for the sake of our instruction he should permit the concreteness of such words, accordingly he employs such human expressions, since it would not otherwise be possible for human hearing to cope with the sublimity of the message had he spoken to us in a manner worthy of the Lord. Let us give good thought to this, and never remain rooted in the ordinariness of the expressions, but make it the occasion for marvelling at his ineffable goodness in showing such considerateness and not spurning the limitations of our nature.[20]

This book aims to help students of the Word imitate in their ministry the divine concern and considerateness that the Scriptures exemplify.

Bibliography

L. Alonso Schökel , *La Palabra Inspirada,* Barcelona: Herder, 1966 (ET, *The Inspired Word,* New York: Herder and Herder, 1965)

L. Bopp, "The salvific power of the Word according to the Church Fathers" in K. Rahner et al, *The Word. Readings in Theology,* New York: Kenedy, 1964

R. E. Brown, *The Critical Meaning of the Bible,* London: Chapman, 1982

D. S. Browning (ed.), *Practical Theology,* San Francisco: Harper and Row, 1983

D. W. Cleverley Ford, *The Ministry of the Word,* London: Hodder and Stoughton, 1979

L. Deiss, *Vivre La Parole en Communauté,* Paris : Desclée, 1974 (ET *God's Word and God's People,* Collegeville: Liturgical, 1976)

---

[20] Homily 50 on *Genesis* (*PG* 54,521).

A. Dulles, *Models of Revelation*, Garden City: Doubleday, 1983.

G. Ebeling, *Dogmatik des Christlichen Glaubens* I, Tubingen: Mohr, 1979

J. Ellul, *La Parole Humiliée*, Paris: Editions du Seuil, 1981 (ET *The Humiliation of the Word*, Grand Rapids: Eerdmans, 1985)

R. C. Hill, "St John Chrysostom and the Incarnation of the Word in Scripture," *Compass Theology Review* 14 (Sept.1980) 34-38

A. Léonard, *La Parole de Dieu en Jesus Christ*, Tournai: Casterman, 1961

G. Moran, *Theology of Revelation*, New York: Herder and Herder, 1967

G. Panikulam, *Koinonia in the New Testament*, Rome: Biblicum, 1979

O. Semmelroth, *Wirkendes Wort*, Frankfurt am Main: Verlag Josef Knecht, 1962 (ET *The Preaching Word*, New York: Herder and Herder, 1965)

E. & J. Whitehead, *Method in Ministry. Theological Reflection and Christian Ministry*, New York: Seabury, 1981

Enchridion Biblicum, Rome: Editiones Arnodo, 1961, 4th ed.

Practical exercises for ministry

1. Reflect on what the various forms of Christian tradition have to say about the role of the Word in the Christian community: doctrinal tradition (in the Creeds, e.g.), liturgical tradition (in the way the Word is spoken and heard in the liturgy), scriptural tradition (use a concordance for usage of Word of God, scripture). Does the lived experience of the community correspond with that tradition?

2. By using a concordance (under "scripture(s)") and a NT Introduction (for patristic statement), examine what light the New Testament and the Fathers throw on the way the Word of God came to be enshrined in a written text, what the function of this text was, and how it shared in the saving purpose of the ministry of the Word.

3. Keep an attentive eye for the way ministers of the Word - preachers, teachers, catechists - speak of revelation, and analyse their models of revelation for adequacy as a basis for ministry of the Word. Is there any tendency in their/your usage to distinguish Scripture from sacraments and not regard Scripture itself as sacramental? What is lost by so doing? Is the phrase "Word and sacrament" helpful?

4. Examine your own upbringing at home, in your parish, in your initial and further Christian education from the viewpoint of biblical tradition: how far were you introduced at appropriate stages to the bread of life in the Scriptures? What adjustments would need to be made to achieve the ideal of *Dei Verbum* Ch.6?

Chapter Two

Readiness for the Word

Outline

Acceptance of the Incarnation and adoption of an adequate theology of
revelation lead ministers of the Word to consider also the condition of
the recipient of that Word from the viewpoint of

- the readiness of individuals for the Scriptures
- the findings of developmental scientists on stages of growth
- patristic and magisterial statement on fidelity both to the Word and its
  recipients.

1. For whom the bread is broken

The ministry of the Word is exercised within the process of
revelation that we know as *koinonia*, a sharing of divine life that
occurs in both the historical Incarnation and the scriptural Word.
In Chapter One we looked at the way this sharing, this
relationship is affected by the nature of that incarnate Word. As
well as considering the gift and its giver, however, the bread to be
broken, we need advert to those to whom the gift is given and for
whom the bread is broken; *koinonia*, relationship, fellowship,
sharing, communion requires an active recipient, not simply a
generous donor. The whole biblical message is an offer of life that
calls for response: "My word shall not return to me empty," vows
the Lord; the earth is meant to bring forth and sprout (Is 55.10-
11).

In the past it has happened that the Word has come but has
not been received, and the gift has been squandered, the bread of
life has not been accepted. Reverence for the text of the Word has
not always been accompanied by respect for the condition and

needs of those to whom the Word is directed, their gifts, abilities, capacities, background, levels of attainment, age, sex, mentality - in short, **their state of readiness.** Children have not infrequently been treated as adults by preachers and catechists, and given large slabs of sophisticated biblical material from an oriental culture without regard for their capacity to appreciate it; adults, on the other hand, have been lectured on biblical topics without the possibility of personally responding to the inspired text in properly adult models of learning. Ministers of the Word have not always been acquainted with contemporary learning theories that suggest taking account of the listeners' world view and the knowledge they already possess. Nor have they capitalised on the findings of the human sciences that treat of development of people in their readiness to receive the message.

Yet even on theological grounds it is the condition of the recipient of the Word, the listener, the reader, to which the minister should be sensitive. The *koinonia* that the Scriptures represent is not something magical, automatic, inhuman, with no regard for the condition of the recipients; the very existence of the biblical composers and the sacred writings attest to that - human events, human agents, human processes. From his infancy the Word made flesh was likewise at the mercy of those to whom he came: some were not ready, and knew him not; others, believing in his name, accepted him and were given power to become children of God. As an adult, a Jewish male of the first century, his impact then and later has differed with the attitudes, expectations, racial background, age, sex, receptivity generally of listeners and readers of the Good News. Predictably, this *koinonia* has in God's wisdom not been an unqualified success, but it has demonstrated something critical for the ministry of the Word - **acceptance of and respect for diversity in people.** The News does not prove Good for the recipients unless they are in a condition to receive it.

As the Incarnation suggests, God does not rush people; the Man of Sorrows had himself first to be the Babe of Bethlehem. No point in providing solid food in place of milk if people are not ready for it (cf 1 Cor 3.3). Readiness is critical to acceptance and appreciation. The patristic educators understood this truth in regard to acceptance of the Word in the plan of salvation. Chrysostom reminds his congregation in Antioch:

> When Moses in the beginning took on the instruction of mankind, he taught his listeners the elements, whereas Paul and John, taking over from Moses, could at that later stage transmit more developed notions. Hence we discover the reason for the considerateness (*synkatabasis*) shown to date, namely, that under the guidance of the Spirit he was speaking in a manner appropriate to his hearers as he outlined everything.[1]

The **divine considerateness for human readiness** that the Scriptures exemplify should characterise the ministry of God's Word. Chrysostom takes a leaf out of his own book:

> What is the use of proving God's immunity from suffering to the person who doesn't believe he exercises any providence, or cares for things that exist, or even exists himself? So first of all talk to them about those things, and when they have got the idea of God's existence, gradually refine their thinking, lead them to the fulness of belief, talk to them of more exalted matters, and introduce the question of God's immunity from suffering.[2]

Augustine, too, in lecturing on the ministry of the Word in the light of his own experience in that ministry, enunciates the same principle: always speak **"with respect for the listener's capacity and resources"** (*pro capacitate ac viribus audientis*).[3] He had good reason to know that people come to the Word from a vast range of backgrounds, needs, capacities, states of readiness, and that adaptation (considerateness) is thus a first principle in ministering to them. Like Chrysostom he can speak from his own experience:

> My own experience has been that I react differently when I see before me for instruction learned or ignorant, fellow citizen or stranger, rich or poor, man in the street or dignitary, a person of this or that family, this or that age or sex, coming from one sect or another, one heresy or another. My instruction begins,

---

[1] Homily 2 on *Genesis* (PG 53,29).
[2] Homily on *Psalm* VI (PG 55,71).
[3] *De Catechizandis Rudibus* 7,11 (PL 40,317).

proceeds and concludes differently depending on my reaction to them.[4]

The Christian educator adapts his message to the condition of readiness of those to whom he is ministering.

2. Findings of the human sciences on readiness

The necessity of this basic principle of the ministry of the Word, arising from a theological consideration of the Incarnation and divine *koinonia*, as well as from the insights and practice of scriptural authors and early educators, has in more recent times been reinforced by the findings of theorists, researchers and practitioners of the human sciences, particularly on human development and learning processes. Their work has had a profound effect on education generally, including religious education; in brief, they have confirmed that incarnational need for acceptance of and respect for diversity in people and for **recognition of their stage of development.**

This has emerged from all the areas of study of **developmental researchers**: human development generally, with particular treatment of cognitive development, moral development, faith development, religious development. The principal scholars contributing to these studies hail from France, Denmark, the United States, England; their findings have had an effect on education world-wide, even if they have had their critics and reservations have been held about the universal applicability of their findings outside European cultures, to women equally as to men, etc. Their value for the ministry of the Word is that they insist uniformly on acceptance of that principle of recognising the degree of readiness for the Word on the part of the recipient - something that came to Chrysostom and Augustine via intuition, experience and theologising.

---

[4] *Ibid.*, 15,23 (*PL* 40,328).

The inspiration for later developmentalists' work was given by psychologists Erik Erikson and Jean Piaget, who earlier this century researched **human development** generally and **cognitive development** respectively. For both, the human being develops through a series of stages or 'crises' or turning points that are invariant and sequential - Erikson in regard to psycho-social maturation and Piaget studying the cognitive. For **Erikson** a human being moves from infancy and childhood through adolescence to adulthood and maturity by means of eight stages: trust, autonomy, initiative, industry, identity, intimacy, generativity, integrity - the attainment of each stage involving a balance of opposites (e.g., trust and mistrust, intimacy and isolation) and intersecting with social form and expectations. **Piaget** concentrated on the psychology of the child in tracing the way people come to knowledge, moving to an ability to handle an increasing number of variables and escape an egocentric viewpoint - decentration, in Piaget's terminology. In the light of these developmentalists' work, educators could see the need to view human development and learning as a process and adjust their educative efforts to the particular stage of a person's development.

In the wake of Piaget's observations about children's changing attitudes to rules, further research into moral development was conducted by Lawrence **Kohlberg**, who distinguished three levels of development: pre-conventional morality, conventional morality, and post-conventional morality. Kohlberg was interested not in behaviour but, like Piaget, in cognition, and he advanced a sequence of six stages of **a developing moral reasoning** within the three levels: obedience and punishment, self-interest; conformity, law and order; social contract, universal principles. Kohlberg held that the moral reasoning of a person at one stage cannot be comprehended by a person whose moral reasoning is more than one stage removed: if my motto is "me first", I will have difficulty comprehending the stance of a person for whom duty is "stern daughter of the voice of God", as it was for Wordsworth. And if you are Christian educator, minister of God's moral message, you will need to be alert to the stages of moral development of your listeners, or suffer the fate of not being understood. As Augustine's experience told him, "Much depends on what the matter in hand suggests and what the audience present indicate not only what they can take but are even keen to hear."[5]

More recently, under the influence of this earlier developmental work, researchers have turned to an area even more germane to the ministry of the Word, **growth in faith**. Beginning with human faith, though himself a believer, James **Fowler** in the last two decades has been articulating a series of stages of faith development that reflect clearly Erikson's 'crises' of psycho-social development. They begin with the "intuitive-projective faith" of a child under the age of seven, much under the influence of its parents, and proceed to "universalising faith", which perhaps few of us ever achieve (like Erikson's final stage of integrity). Fowler's terminology is deliberately resistant to simplistic paraphrase, but his stages of development can perhaps be translated thus: experienced faith, affiliative faith, conventional faith, personal faith, community faith, universal faith. His thinking, related to Erikson's stages of human development, may be outlined thus:

Relationship between Stages in Human Development, Human Faith and Religious Faith[6]

Erikson: Human Development	Fowler: Human Faith Development	Religious Faith Development
	0. Pre-stage. Infancy and undifferentiated faith	0. Childhood Faith
1. Development of Trust Autonomy Initiative	1. Intuitive-Projective Faith	1. Experienced Faith (Imitative Faith)
2. Development of Industry and Self-Confidence	2. Mythic-Literal Faith	2.Affiliative Faith (Joining Faith)

---

[5] *Ibid.*, 26,51 (*PL* 40 ,345).
[6] M. Flynn, *The Effectiveness of Catholic Schools*, 240. Used with permission.

3. Development of Identity	3. Synthetic-Conventional Faith	3. From Conventional to Searching Faith (a group experience of faith)
4. Development of Intimacy	4. Individuative-Reflective Faith	4. Personal Faith
5. Development of Generativity	5. Paradoxical-Consolidative Faith (Conjunctive Faith)	5. Community/Caring Faith (a Rejoining Faith)
6. Development of Integrity	6. Universalising Faith	6. Universal Faith

Though Fowler claims to be describing development of human faith, his work sheds light also on **growth in religious faith**, of which the *General Catechetical Directory* says: "The life of faith passes through various stages just as does our existence while we are attaining maturity and taking on the duties of our life."[7] Education in faith, to which the ministry of the Word contributes, is much dependent on this process of development; for instance, the Church has always been concerned that young people in particular will successfully make that transition from conventional faith to an owned, personal faith, even if this for many occurs via a painful, searching, questioning process - a process which the faith of some people does not survive and which a more adequate ministry of the Word would render less difficult.

A biblical scholar involved in adult education, William G. Thompson, has applied Fowler's findings to study of the New Testament and in particular to the Gospel of Mark. "I am convinced that persons at different faith-stages may read the same story in Mark, but in interacting with it they will find different elements helpful in their search for meaning. Mark's Jesus can be significant for persons at all stages, but they will view him very differently."[8] Thompson suggests that children and others at a stage of 'mythic-literal' faith would find Mark fascinating for its dramatic action, conflict and concrete, sensible images, whereas those who have advanced to a more personal,

---

[7] *Directorium Catechisticum Generale*, Rome: Sacred Congregation for the Clergy, 1971,30.
[8] "Mark's Gospel and faith development," *Chicago Studies* 26 (1987) 140.

'individuative-reflective' faith may look more critically at Mark, demythologising its symbols and metaphors to fit their own radical thinking. For these latter, Mark's Gospel is not a simple story but an account of a cosmic struggle between evil and God's power, Jesus confronting Satan on behalf of the kingdom of God. **The biblical educator** takes account of this development in faith.

In England, some years earlier than Fowler, educationists like Harold Loukes and Ronald Goldman, perhaps also under the influence of Piaget's work on children's cognitive development, had been expressing a widely felt unease about religious education in state schools, where syllabuses were heavily biblical in character (unlike Catholic schools). **Loukes and Goldman** raised the question, What impact has all this biblical study had on the **religious development** of English children, and they found it was very little. Which led them to write books on young people's religious development, such as *Readiness for Religion*,[9] which takes as its cue these lines from poet T. S. Eliot's *The Rock*:

> Where is the life we have lost in living?
> Where is the wisdom we have lost in knowledge?
> Where is the knowledge we have lost in information?

These are questions that can be put to people of all ages, as are Goldman's questions about **readiness for religion**: readiness for learning; intellectual readiness; emotional readiness; physical readiness. He asks, "What aspects of Christianity are children ready to learn at certain stages of their development?" Though Goldman's empirical studies have since been rigorously critiqued, he is in effect paraphrasing Augustine all those years before: "Much depends on what the matter in hand suggests and what the audience present indicate not only what they can take but are even keen to hear." The question of readiness - *pro capacitate ac viribus audientis* - is vital to all stages of religious education, including the ministry of the Word.

---

[9] London: Routledge and Kegan Paul, 1965.

3. Learning theories and ministry

To the work of these developmentalists **learning theorists** have added further stimulus to all educators, including ministers of the Word, to address the condition of the learner. They emphasise what may be an obvious truth, that the knowledge people already possess is a principal determiner of what they can come to know. In particular, proponents of schema theory suggest that knowledge is not a basket of facts, that **the essence of knowledge is structure**, that substantial differences in comprehension, learning and memory occur when the learner is able to bring to bear a more developed schema, or structure of information. The minister of the Word, for instance, may be able to bring the reader of *Genesis* to greater appreciation of primeval history if there has already been treatment of the question of authorship in the ancient world; and New Testament students with an historical background will better realise that the Cornelius who led "the Italian band" in *Acts* 10.1 was rather an officer than a musician. We saw Chrysostom respecting this principle above in gradually introducing neophytes to the attributes of God.

For other theorists, like David Ausubel, meaningful learning occurs when **advance organisers** or structured overviews of knowledge are provided to bridge the gap between what the learners already know and what they need to know before they can successfully learn the task at hand. I can, for instance, capitalise on my class's familiarity with the processes of folk literature to lead them to an understanding of multiple, pseudepigraphical authorship of biblical Torah and Wisdom.

4. A double fidelity

So the theology of the Word and the findings of developmental sciences and learning theories are at one in recommending attention to the readiness of people **at all stages of the evangelising process**. There is a danger of misjudging the appropriate stage at which to introduce people to the Bible, as there is of withholding it from them. Young people going through

a period of 'searching faith' may not be the right soil for solid
biblical education. Those whose moral reasoning is still at an early
stage may not appreciate the point Job is trying to make to his
friends about retribution. Scriptural textbooks for children should
remind them of relevant experiences of their own before
introducing them to the problems of the biblical characters. It
should not be presumed readers of the Bible are in touch with the
culture of biblical peoples. And so on.

Small wonder that major statements of the Church's
magisterium on religious education in recent decades have
laboured the point of a double fidelity on the part of those engaged
in the various ministries of the Word - **fidelity to God**, or the
evangelical message, on the one hand, and on the other **fidelity to
man**, to people. Paul VI says in *Evangelii Nuntiandi*:

> This fidelity both to a message whose servants we are and to the
> people to whom we must transmit it living and intact is the
> central axis of evangelisation.[10]

This apostolic letter (and the 1974 Synod on evangelisation it was
commenting on) was devoted to examining how well the Church
today is equipped to "put the Gospel into people's hearts with
conviction, freedom of spirit and effectiveness" (#4), and it
devotes much attention to "the beneficiaries of evangelisation". Its
principle of double fidelity in the ministry of the Word is
emphasised also in the document *The Renewal of the Education of
Faith* (originating with the Italian episcopacy and) recommended
by Paul VI for the whole Church and adopted with supplements by
many national episcopacies:

> The fundamental law of all catechetical method is that of fidelity
> to the Word of God and fidelity to the concrete needs of the
> faithful. This is the ultimate criterion by which catechists must
> appraise their work as educators. This is the fundamental
> inspiration of every proposal for renewal - fidelity to God and
> fidelity to man... It is the attitude of the charity of Christ, the
> Word of God made flesh.[11]

---

10 *AAS* 68 (1976) 7.
11 *The Renewal of the Education of Faith*, Sydney: Dwyer, 1970, #160.

It is what John Paul II, in his apostolic letter *Catechesi Tradendae* following the 1977 Synod, insisted:

> The plurality of methods in contemporary catechesis can be a sign of vitality and ingenuity. In any case, the method chosen must ultimately be referred to a law that is fundamental for the whole of the Church's life: fidelity to God and fidelity to man in a single loving attitude.[12]

In regard to the former fidelity, religious educators have observed **the various languages of faith**, or languages of the Church, in which the message is expressed, of which recitation of the biblical story is but one. In addition there is the theological language of dogmatic formulae, the liturgical language of the rites of worship, the language of witness of Christian living that can be perceived in the facts of the life of the Church - all contributing to a fidelity to the divine message.[13] But more to our point here is that necessary concomitant fidelity to the recipient of the message. This itself calls for a variety of languages on the part of the minister, communicating appropriately as need and readiness require; Paul himself was sensitive to the relative appropriateness of meat and milk: "I fed you with milk, not solid food; for you were not ready for it; and even yet you are not ready, for you are still of the flesh" (1 Cor 3.2).

It is a necessary fidelity - a "law fundamental for the whole of the Church's life," in the words of John Paul II - though we would have to admit that the ministry of the Word has not always respected it, preferring instead to concentrate on fidelity to the Word (while neglecting implications of incarnation which that very Word exemplifies). It is a **fidelity to the whole person**: just as Paul VI sees the message being transmitted "living and intact", so the ministry of the Word ideally takes account of all aspects of the living personality of the recipients - intellectual, yes, but also sensual, emotional, social, aesthetic, spiritual (not to mention cultural, something to be explored in the next chapter); from the

---

[12] *AAS* 71 (1979) 1323.
[13] Cf J. Colomb, *Le service de l'évangile* I, 98-99.

beginning people have responded to the Word incarnate in all these aspects of their being, just as the scriptural Word itself appeals to spirit and imagination as well as cognitive faculties, to symbolic as well as rational thinking. It is a fidelity to the ways in which the human spirit acts and is affected, taking account of the influence of people's milieu, the role of experience in learning, the need for relevance to the real, subjective interests of the learner, the need for respecting the learner's models of thought, for respecting individuality.[14] Recent developments in biblical and theological study, such as a feminist hermeneutic, the theology of story, the role of imagination in theology, reflect such fidelity to the human spirit.

Our discharge of the ministry of the Word, therefore, likewise reflects this double fidelity. As educational psychologists and learning theorists profit from the findings of the developmentalists, we take advantage of the insights of the human sciences along with theological principles to realise that teaching and learning occur at various levels. With Augustine we admit that much depends on the age, sex, mentality of the recipients , that we must in our ministry plumb their needs, their abilities, their state of readiness generally, the situation in which they live and we find them.

It is not simply a question of development; **freedom is also involved,** as Paul VI realised in stating the Church's aim in evangelisation as putting the Gospel in people's hearts not only with conviction but also with "freedom of spirit". Religious educationists, not to mention contextual theologians, have raised the question of how free people are to accept the message - psychologically, politically, culturally free. Education in faith must come to terms with familial, social, and cultural conditions impinging upon the individual's freedom of response - such as oppressive institutions, the way language structures consciousness, cultural tradition, and other controlling forces in the environment that affect human behaviour. The minister of the Word must do all possible to ensure that when the Word comes to his own, his own will be enabled to receive him.

---

[14] *Ibid., passim.*

Bibliography

R. C. Anderson, "Some reflections on the acquisition of knowledge," *Educational Research* 13 (1984 No.9) 5-10

D. Ausubel, *The Psychology of Meaningful Verbal Learning*, New York: Grune and Stratton, 1963

P. Babin, *Les Jeunes et la foi*, Lyons: Editions du Chalet, 1960 (ET *Crisis of faith. The Religious Psychology of Adolescence*, Dublin: Gill, 1963)

K. Barker, *Religious Education, Catechesis and Freedom*, Birmingham Al: Religious Education Press, 1981

C. Brüsselmans et al, *Toward Moral and Religious Maturity,* Morristown NJ: Silver Burdett, 1980

J. Colomb, *Le service de l'évangile*, 2 vols, Paris: Desclée, 1968

J. W. Fowler, *Stages of Faith. The Psychology of Human Development and the Quest for Meaning*, San Francisco: Harper and Row, 1981

M. Flynn, *Catholic Schools and the Communication of Faith*, Sydney: St Paul, 1979

N. L. Gage, D. C. Berliner, *Educational Psychology*, Dallas: Houghton Mifflin, 1984, 3rd ed.

R. Goldman, *Readiness for Religion. A Basis for Developmental Religious Education*, London: Routledge and Kegan Paul, 1965

M. Harris, *Teaching and Religious Imagination: An Essay in the Theology of Teaching*, San Francisco: Harper and Row, 1987

J. Hofinger (ed.), *Katechetik Heute*, Freiburg: Herder, 1961 (ET *Teaching All Nations*, Freiburg: Herder, 1961)

J. Jungmann, *Die Frohbotschaft und Unsere Glaubensverkundigung*, Regensburg: Pustet, 1936 (ET *The Good News Yesterday and Today*, New York: Sadlier, 1962)

L. Kohlberg, "Stages of moral development as a basis for moral education" in C. M. Beck et al (edd.), *Moral Education. Interdisciplinary Approaches*, New York: Newman, 1971

J. McIntyre, *Faith, Theology and Imagination*, Edinburgh: The Handsell Press, 1987

G. Moran, *Interplay: A Theory of Religion and Education*, Winona: St Mary's, 1981

J. Piaget, *L'épistémologie génétique*, Paris: Presses Universitaires de France, 1970 (ET *The Principle of Genetic Epistemology*, London: Routledge and Kegan Paul, 1972)

M. P. Riccards, "The structure of religious development. Empirical evidence for a stage theory," *Lumen Vitae* (Eng.ed.) 33 (1978 No.1) 97-123

E. Schüssler Fiorenza, *Bread Not Stone. The Challenge of Feminist Biblical Interpretation*, Boston: Beacon Press, 1984

A Vergote, *Godsdienstpsychologie*, Tielt: Lannoo, 1967 (TF *Psychologie religieuse*, Brussels: Charles Dessart; ET *The Religious Man. A Psychological Study of Religious Attitudes*, Dublin: Gill and Macmillan, 1969)

relevant journals: *British Journal of Religious Education*
            The Living Light
            Lumen Vitae
            PACE
(Bibliographical information on any journal can be found in the standard catalogues such as *Ulrich's International Periodical Directory* or *Religious and Inspirational Books and Serials in Print.*)

Practical exercises for ministry

1. Think of instances where factors such as age, sex, race, education affect the receptivity of a group or individuals within a group to the Scriptures. For example, how would you plan to present *Judges* 19 to a group of women? Take other particular examples.

2. Have you begun to think of the question of how the Bible fits into the education of children? What were your own experiences as a child, can you recall? Does Paul's analogy of milk and solid food (applied by him to adults, admittedly) have any relevance? Select two or three parts of the Bible suited to children, and plan the way you would present them. (The matter will be raised more precisely in Part II.)

3. Can you parallel Augustine's experience in adjusting your ministry to the different people you encounter? Or do you think you could be guilty of concentrating more on the Word and neglecting the particular condition of the listeners? Take particular instances, real or imagined, and examine them for 'double fidelity'. On the other hand, do you feel you have had similar consideration shown to you in your experience of the ministry of the Word?

4. How do the findings of developmentalists apply to your particular ministry? Do stages of growth in moral reasoning, faith, religion have implications for your work with individuals or groups? Be specific.

Chapter Three

The Word incarnate in various cultures

Outline

Fidelity to the Word and to those to whom it is addressed requires consideration of the cultural conditioning affecting both:

- the scriptural Word, like Jesus, bears the imprint of cultural origins;

- we come to the Word in our own culture: for us the message needs a fresh inculturation;

- teaching and learning the Scriptures take account of different cultural backgrounds.

1. God's Word culturally conditioned

Incarnation, enfleshment in the human condition or in a medium such as language and literature, involves limitation, specificity. This process of commitment to the particular can be both enriching and constraining. Jesus' commitment to our human condition means **his acceptance of the limitations,** the strengths and weaknesses, of the particular cultural situation of his birth. Vatican II's decree on missionary activity depends on this truth as its first principle: "Christ himself by his incarnation confined himself to the precise social and cultural conditions of the people with whom he lived."[1] This acceptance of limitation by the redeemer of the universe may seem paradoxical, but it is exactly that which distinguishes the Christian economy.[2]

---

[1] *Ad Gentes* 10.
[2] Cf John Paul II to the Pontifical Biblical Commission, *AAS* 71 (1979) 608, on this paradox.

It was the will of the Son of God to be a Jew of Nazareth of Galilee, who spoke Aramaic, who was subject to pious parents of Israel... Jesus grows up in the midst of the practices and institutions of the Palestine of the first century, learning trades of his time, observing the behaviour of fishermen, peasants and merchants of his society... Nourished on the piety of Israel, formed by the instruction of the Law and the Prophets, to which a quite singular experience of God as Father permits him to bring an unparalleled depth, Jesus is situated in a spiritual tradition deeply entrenched, that of Hebrew prophetism. Like the prophets of an earlier age, he is the mouth of God and call to conversion. His style is just as typical: his vocabulary, literary genres, stylistic devices, all suggest the lineage of Elijah and Elisha - biblical parallelism, proverbs, paradoxes, admonitions, beatitudes and even symbolic actions.[3]

Obviously, these conditions of history, race and language represented, and continue to represent, a problem for some who would approach Jesus from within a different culture.

Likewise in his scriptural incarnation the Word comes to us with a cultural conditioning arising from the literary, linguistic, historical, geographical, social, religious background of composers raised in civilisations different from our own. **Culture** itself can be defined variously, and Vatican II's *Gaudium et Spes* admitted as much before observing: "Various conditions of community living, as well as various patterns for organising the goods of life, arise from diverse ways of using things, of labouring, of expressing oneself, of practising religion, of forming customs, of establishing laws and juridical institutions, of advancing the arts and sciences, and of promoting beauty" (#53).

In these terms the world of the composers of the Old and New Testaments differs significantly from our own, as Jesus' world does. Ministers of the Word **take account of such cultural differences**, as biblical critics have enabled them to do. As John Paul II told the Pontifical Biblical Commission in 1979, "the Mesopotamian cultures, those of Egypt, Canaan, Persia, the

---

[3] International Theological Commission, "Fede e inculturazione," *La Civiltà Cattolica* 3326 (1989) 165-66.

Hellenistic culture and, for the New Testament, the Greco-Roman culture and that of late Judaism rendered service, day after day, to the revelation of his ineffable mystery of salvation, as your present plenary session makes clear."[4] Some have spoken of the mythological character of biblical material, and have urged us to strip this away by a process of demythologising; others have seen the danger in trying to remove cultural conditioning, just as it would be false to attempt to prise Jesus from his native situation. One such critic warns:

> Demythologisation can also mean the removal of myth as a vehicle of religious expression and the substitution of science and morals. In this sense demythologisation must be strongly rejected. It would deprive religion of its language; it would silence the experience of the holy. Symbols and myths cannot be criticised simply because they are symbols. They must be criticised on the basis of their power to express what they are supposed to express, namely, in this instance, the New Being in Jesus as the Christ.[5]

Better to situate Jesus and the scriptural Word within their cultural origins and help believers appreciate the difference from their own.

2. The culturally conditioned situation of the recipient

Today's believers, too, stand within their own culture, their own "way of life and world view which are held in common by members of the community and are transmitted with conviction to the next generation," their own symbol system;[6] we have our own myths, in other words. **We do not come to the incarnate Word culture-free**; in fact, culture with all its ramifications can inhibit our freedom of response, or at least influence the nature and expression of our response and distinguish it from the response of believers in another culture. Witness the artistic response of

---

[4] *AAS* 71 (1979) 607.

[5] P. Tillich , *Systematic Theology* II , London: James Nisbet & Co, 1957, 176. Tillich's point remains valid even if his use of "myth" in places would not go unchallenged.

[6] K. Barker, *Religious Education, Catechesis and Freedom*, Birmingham Al: Religious Education Press, 1981, 160.

artists in contemporary Latin America to the Gospel accounts of
the crucifixion (as collected, for example, in Hans-Ruedi Weber's
On A Friday Noon [7]), compare these tortured portraits with the
relatively comfortable crucified Cristo of an Old Master, and note
how conditions of deprivation and oppression evoke a markedly
different response to the scriptural text. Christian
anthropologists, too, suggest the parable of the Sower could be
interpreted culturally to make the point that "the divine call meets
a ground, *already present*, characterised by certain conditions,
qualifications and reservations, with its freedom conditioned in
various ways."[8] The preacher and teacher of the Bible would do
well to discern, not only the cultural conditioning of the Word, but
as well the effect on the recipient of his or her own culture.

Can we recognise these **cultural features** conditioning
reception of the Word? Of course, there are those that parallel the
composers' own situation - factors of history, geography, race,
language and the like. Can the minister of the Word go further
and descry the concerns that readers and listeners **in today's
societies** bring to the biblical message, thrown up by our modern
culture(s)? There is surely a sensitivity to human rights and
discrimination that did not consistently preoccupy the biblical
composers; in particular, there is today a feminist viewpoint and
reaction to sexist attitudes and language that escaped biblical
composers and patristic commentators alike. Listeners and
readers of the Word in modern culture are also conditioned to
respond better to audiovisual means of communication than to a
'hot', mono-medium form; with children in some societies looking
at television for as much as forty hours a week,[9] *kerygma* has to
take on a new meaning: the spoken Word no longer suffices.
Processing, recording and retrieving information through
computers and data banks in this technetronic age bear no
resemblance to the systems employed by our forebears (not to
mention the biblical composers).

---

[7] London: SPCK, 1979.

[8] L. Rulla, *Anthropology of the Christian Vocation. I Interdisciplinary Bases*, 284.

[9] Cf J. Holman, *The Impact of Television during Early Childhood* (Australian Early
Childhood Research Booklets 5), Canberra: AEC Association, 1980, 2.

Another feature of **our modern world** is the vast gap between underdeveloped and (over?)developed nations: poverty, deprivation, oppression keep the Third World in thrall, whereas in other 'Worlds' their plight and liberation from it are at least notionally an issue (made possible by that network of AV communications). Also brought to the forefront of media attention is the effect of technology on the world's eco-system; conservation and global responsibility are live issues for those suffering from nuclear fallout and the ravages of war, the greenhouse effect, pollution. Today's world is a vastly more secularised one by comparison with the biblical world - 'post-Christian' in the view of some, for whom God (if not dead) is at least absent. It is also a world that is pluralist in its values and beliefs, despite the possibilities of communications to achieve some consensus. Youth, in developed countries at least, have given rise to a subculture of their own, with distinctive idioms and interests.

Such are some of **the cultural features of today's world** that in varying degrees condition the response of listeners to the Word. If discerning them challenges the minister, respecting them in ministry is a keener challenge.

3. The need for inculturation

In breaking the bread of the Word, how does the minister respond to the cultural conditioning of the recipients? **By imitating the divine considerateness**, *synkatabasis*, that characterises (the Word made flesh and) the scriptural Word in working for inculturation - that is, incarnation - of the Christian message in a particular cultural context in such a way that the Christian experiences transmitted in the Scriptures evoke a response of faith through elements proper to that culture.[10] In this the ministry of the Word is akin to the liturgy and other forms of Christian tradition: we think of African creeds, Melanesian

---

[10] Cf P. Arrupe, "Father General's letter on inculturation to the whole Society of Jesus, 1978" quoted by S. U. Amateze, *The Prophetic Role of the People of God in Evangelisation in the Light of Vatican II*, 92.

liturgies, Latin American theologies - all of which exemplify that necessary double fidelity.

The great **patristic homilists and catechists** came to inculturation intuitively. In commenting on *Psalm* 147 Augustine says of the Church and his own ministry:

> Already the whole body of Christ speaks the languages of all, and those she doesn't yet speak she will. The Church will expand, you see, until she takes over all languages... I am bold enough to tell you, I speak everyone's language. I am in the body of Christ, I am in the Church of Christ; if the body of Christ now speaks everyone's language, I too am familiar with all languages: my language is Greek, my language is Syriac, my language is Hebrew, my language is that of every people because I am to be found in the unity of all peoples.[11]

Of the opening verse of *Psalm* 6, "O Lord, rebuke me not in thy anger, nor chastise me in thy wrath," Chrysostom gives an explanation in terms of a materialistic culture:

> When you hear of God's anger and wrath, don't get the idea of anything typical of man; the words are used out of considerateness for us. The divine nature is free of all these passions. He speaks this way so as to make an impression on the minds of materialistic people. When we speak with foreigners, we use their language; if we speak to children, we babble away with them, and even if we are extremely gifted, we show considerateness (*synkatabainein*) for their undeveloped state. What is surprising in our doing this in words when we do it in actions, like biting our nails and feigning anger, all for the sake of instructing the children? God likewise, wanting to make an impression on materialistic people, made use of such words. For in speaking, his concern was not for his own glory but for the benefit of his listeners.[12]

For Chrysostom the minister of the Word is bound even more to fidelity to the situation of the believer than to respect for divine

---

[11] *PL* 37,1929.
[12] *PG* 55,71.

transcendence - a remarkable concession by this Eastern commentator and preacher.

The magisterium in recent times has reinforced this accent. Study of the Scriptures, says Vatican II on the formation of seminarians in mission countries, "should be combined with an effort to come to grips with the way of thinking and acting peculiar to their own people. So let the minds of the students remain open and attuned to recognise and be able to evaluate the culture of their nation; in their philosophical and theological studies let them discern the bases for relating their ancestral traditions and religious practices to the Christian tradition."[13] **Matteo Ricci**, foiled in his attempt to convert China four centuries ago by Rome's insistence on Latin ways (in the popular interpretation of the incident), would have rejoiced to see his principle of inculturation so formally (if belatedly) adopted. Rome today urges adoption of his approach on the highest authority:

> While he was on earth Christ revealed himself as the perfect communicator. Through his incarnation, he utterly identified himself with those who were to receive his communication, and he gave his message not only in words but in the whole manner of his life. He spoke from within, that is to say, from out of the press of his people. He preached the divine message without fear or compromise. He adjusted to his people's way of talking and to their patterns of thought. And he spoke out of the predicament of their time.[14]

Synods on evangelisation and catechesis in recent years have explored the topic and further reinforced the need for an inculturated ministry of the Word - even if sometimes more cautiously than the Fathers. So Paul VI in his comprehensive statement on evangelisation, *Evangelii Nuntiandi*, following the 1974 Synod:

---

[13] *Ad Gentes* 16.

[14] Pontifical Council for the Instruments of Social Communication, *Communio et Progressio* (Pastoral Instruction on the Means of Social Communication), *AAS* 63 (1971) 597-98.

> The individual churches, intimately built up not only of people but also of aspirations, of riches and limitations, of ways of praying, of loving, of looking at life and the world which distinguish this or that human gathering, have the task of assimilating the essence of the Gospel message and of transposing it, without the slightest betrayal of its essential truth, into the language that these particular people understand, then of proclaiming it in this language. The transposition has to be done with the discernment, seriousness, respect and competence which the matter calls for in the field of liturgical expression, and in the areas of catechesis, theological formulation, secondary ecclesial structures, and ministries. And the word 'language' should be understood less in the semantic or literary sense than in the sense which one may call anthropological and cultural (#63).

The 1977 Synod of Bishops Message to the People of God stressed (more in Chrysostom's manner) the reciprocal advantages of inculturating the message: "Through catechesis the Christian faith must become incarnate in all cultures. A true 'incarnation' of faith through catechesis supposes not only a process of 'giving' but also of 'receiving'"(#5). John Paul II admitted as much in addressing the Pontifical Biblical Commission: "The same divine Word previously became human language, adopting the ways of expression of the different cultures which, from Abraham to the Seer of the Apocalypse, have offered to the adorable mystery of God's salvific love the possibility of making itself accessible and understandable to successive generations, despite the multiple diversity of their historical situations."[15]

Inculturating the scriptural message, far from being a regrettable necessity, is a positive enrichment of it, like a musical composition transposed into a different key. There should be no patronising attitude in our inculturation of Scripture, as there is nothing patronising in that supreme exemplar of inculturation and *synkatabasis* (itself often lazily and wrongly rendered "condescension"), the Incarnation. The Word stands to receive a **fresh impact when thus inculturated,** moving beyond mere

---

[15] *AAS* 71 (1979) 607.

restatement; while continuity of tradition is important, "besides continuity there is development," says Bernard Lonergan. "There is the less conspicuous type of development that arises when the Gospel is preached effectively to a different culture or to a different class in the same culture."[16] Hence the recent statement of the International Theological Commission on inculturation of the Gospel can speak of the benefit of "a fruitful meeting with the modern world":

> The inculturation of the Gospel in modern societies will require a methodical effort of research and concerted action. Such effort will presume in those responsible for evangelisation   1) an attitude of acceptance and critical discernment,   2) the capacity to perceive the spiritual expectations and human aspirations of the new cultures,   3) the capacity for cultural analysis with a view to a fruitful meeting with the modern world.[17]

Hence, at least at the level of principle (if not yet in practical detail), the contemporary Church is agreed on the need for an inculturated message.

4. Teaching and learning in various cultures

So the ministers of the Word proceed confidently and enthusiastically to deal with the challenge of incarnating the Word in the culture in which they find themselves. On theological, epistemological and educational grounds they make the necessary transposition to ensure **the proper relationship** between the Word enfleshed in its manifold context (limiting and enriching together) and its culturally conditioned recipients (themselves limited and enriched by those conditions). Making that relationship is part of the process of teaching and learning the Scriptures, and is required in all ministerial situations, culture (in our wide sense) being an aspect of all human life.

We have seen **learning theorists** speaking of schemata, or organised knowledge of the world, as the basis for

---

[16] *Method in Theology*, London: DLT, 1971, 352.
[17] *La Civiltà Cattolica* 3326 (1989) 175.

comprehending, learning and remembering the ideas contained in stories and texts. The knowledge a person already possesses is, in their view, a principal determiner of what a person can come to know. **Knowledge**, in turn, **is conditioned by culture**, so that a person's culture determines in a major way the knowledge he or she can acquire.[18]   Such a learning theory has much to contribute to the ministry of the Word to those of us (particularly in the West) not steeped in the culture(s) of the Bible. With our different traditions of hospitality how are we to appreciate fully the Old Testament's implicit insistence on that attitude (in Abraham, for instance)? how understand its stress on the significance of anointing (whether merely utilitarian, as in the *Song of Songs*, or of deeper import in the Former Prophets), on the retractability of paternal blessings, and so on? One can realise how cultures different from our own, and perhaps in our view more primitive, such as those of Central Africa, could respond more adequately than we to ancient oriental texts presuming acquaintance with polygamy, slavery, sacrifice, kingship, the practice of blessing and cursing, systems for revenge or 'pay-back', casting out evil spirits, corporate responsibility, communication through dreams and visions.[19]   In our preaching, commentary and exegesis we need to introduce our audience to **the cultural differences of the biblical composers.**

This truth about teaching and learning in various cultures has obvious implications for the ministry of the Word also at the humble level of **translation of texts**, as the Bible Societies have long realised. Translators in Papua New Guinea, for instance, have had to cope with rendering "God forgives" in local terms, "God doesn't hang up jawbones." A literal rendering of *Romans* 14.7, "none of us lives to himself, and none of us dies to himself," has been interpreted by many Africans as being a direct confirmation of black magic, because death is almost never regarded by them as natural but is thought to result from the malevolent influence of witchcraft. Other phrases like "bowels of mercy", "circumcised of heart", "girding up the loins of the mind"

---

[18] Cf R. C. Anderson, "Some reflections on the acquisition of knowledge," *Educational Researcher* 13 (1984 November) 8.

[19] E. A. Nida, W.D. Reyburn, *Meaning Across Cultures*, New York: Orbis, 1981, 27-28.

have caused similar problems,[20] and our own Western students and congregations cannot be presumed to understand such terms automatically, either.

At a more elevated level of response to social patterns, many of us have had the experience of introducing an unreceptive group of ladies to Paul's household codes in *Colossians* and *Ephesians*, and endeavouring to explain that the apparent downgrading of women in these passages is merely part of the society of the times somewhat uncritically incorporated into his letters by a busy apostle. The significance of Jesus' conversation with the Samaritan woman at the well in *John* 4 also requires reference to **contemporary social patterns** that discouraged such relative intimacy in a rabbi. More generally, as we have remarked, a patriarchal culture infusing the pages of the Bible requires explication and encourages a re-reading if we in our more egalitarian society are to gain an adequate picture of the world behind the text.[21]

The whole question of **authorship of the biblical writings** needs explanation in terms of cultural conditioning, especially to modern audiences and readers drilled in the technology of immediate record and replay. Composition of Torah, proverbs and psalms extending over centuries, with the involvement of many contributors, is something we are not accustomed to envisage. Differing degrees of Pauline involvement in *Galatians*, *Ephesians* and the Pastorals is also a challenge for today's culturally conditioned readers. Likewise the provenance of compositions of earlier ages we have to struggle to recover; the differing conditions at Antioch and Rome, Ephesus and Alexandria as the context in which biblical composition originated are now strange to us, so that we have to work to overcome this additional cultural barrier in our teaching and learning about the Word.

Then there is the fascination of our culture with the facts of a story, sometimes to the neglect of its truth; as modern

---

[20] *Ibid.*, 1-4.

[21] Katharine Doob Sakenfeld, "Feminist perspectives on Bible and Theology. An Introduction to selected issues and literature," *Interpretation* 42 (1988) 5-18.

Australian biographer Alan Marshall says, "I try to get **beyond the facts to the truth** ." We tend to look in biblical texts for facts where truth alone is available; so we have trouble with primeval history in *Genesis*, with apocalyptic generally, even with the theological cast of history in the Former Prophets. Our initial response is culturally conditioned. Yet our modern world is not without examples of truth being obscured by manipulation of statistics; we can alert our listeners to instances of this kind to illustrate the concerns of the biblical composers.

Our culture likewise constitutes an obstacle to our encounter with the Word in **biblical types of writing,** and even in the **language** of the composers. Popes and Councils have had to remind us that, if we want to understand what the biblical composers intended, we must pay attention to "the customary ways of thinking, speaking and narrating in their culture, as well as to the customs people at that time usually followed in dealing with one another" (*Dei Verbum* 12) . The suggestion has been made that, in place of the bare text of the Bible, what we need is a combination of translation and commentary, in the manner of the Targums provided for Jewish readers who in the post-exilic period could no longer understand Hebrew[22] - such is the distance, not simply linguistically but wholly culturally, between the biblical authors' time and our own.

5. Conclusion

Hence the importance of **an informed and sensitive ministry** of the Word: informed as to the nature and origins of the biblical text and sensitive to the situation of today's believer. Luke shows Paul giving a fine example of such considerate (not "condescending") ministry in bringing the message of salvation to Jews at Pisidian Antioch in terms of Old Testament traditions (*Acts* 13), whereas at Athens in an address to the pagan Areopagus he recasts his message to begin from "the unknown God" (*Acts* 17). If the Church continues to exercise such a ministry, we can say with Augustine, "Come with us as far as the Church has advanced

---

[22] Nida and Reyburn, *Meaning Across Cultures*, 23.

so as to arrive with us where she has not yet advanced. I am bold enough to tell you, I speak everyone's language. I am in the body of Christ... she speaks the languages of all peoples." This confidence in a truly catholic community shown by Augustine the African is characteristically unqualified. The long period between his statements and those of the contemporary Church, however, and the well documented instances of cultural insensitivity in the meantime, suggest we have a way to go in ensuring that the bread of the Word is broken in a way that is palatable to all.

Bibliography

S. U. Amateze [Nigeria], *The Prophetic Role of the People of God in Evangelisation in the Light of Vatican II*, Rome: Pont.Uni.Urbaniana, 1988

P. Arrupe, "Catechesis and 'Inculturation'" in P. S. De Achutegui, J. L. Roche (edd.), *Word, Memory, Witness. The 1977 Bishops' Synod on Catechesis*, Manila: Loyola, 1978

P. Babin, M. McLuhan, *Autre homme, autre chrétien a l'âge électronique*, Lyon: Ed. du Chalet, 1977

International Theological Commission, "Fede e inculturazione," *La Civiltà Cattolica* 3326 (1989) 158-77

J. Martins (ed.), *L'Annuncio del Vangelo Oggi. Commento all'Esortazione Apostolica di Paolo VI, Evangelii Nuntiandi*, Rome: Pont.Uni.Urbaniana, 1977

L. Rulla, *Anthropology of the Christian Vocation. I Interdisciplinary Bases*, Rome: Gregorian University Press, 1986

L. M. Russell (ed.), *Feminist Interpretation of the Bible*, Philadelphia: Westminster, 1985

G. W. Trompf, *The Gospel is not Western*, Maryknoll: Orbis, 1987

M. Warren (ed.), *Source Book for Modern Catechetics*, Winona: St Mary's Press, 1983

United States Catholic Conference, *Faith and culture. A Multicultural Resource*, Washington: USCC, 1987 articles on "Catequesis y Culturas," *Medellin* 61 (March 1990); on inculturation in *Indian Missiological Review* 12 (1990 No.1)

relevant journals: *Word Event*
                      Dei Verbum
                      Teaching All Nations
                      East Asian Pastoral Review
                      Pro Mundi Vita
                      Catechetics in India
                      Vidya Jyoti
                      Medellin

Practical exercises for ministry

1. Set yourself the task of discerning the principal features of the culture (or subculture) of those to whom you are ministering. Then ponder the implications of these cultural features for the way you will approach your ministry of the Word. How *multi*cultural is the community to whom you minister?

2. The Scriptures themselves have in our day been found to enshrine a patriarchal viewpoint that conditions the text and affects modern readers of it. Commentators on the text among the Fathers were also less responsive to the sexual diversity of their congregations than we would prefer. How sensitive to this issue are we in our ministry of the Word? Select a scriptural passage that requires particularly sensitive handling in this regard.

3. Select a body of biblical literature (e.g., Former Prophets, Pastoral Epistles, Wisdom books, patriarchal narratives), and scrutinise the text for instances of particular cultural conditioning. Then consider ways of achieving an adequate transfer of the biblical message in these texts to the culture of those to whom you minister the Word.

4. The youth in any (Western) society can be classed as a subculture within that society, with peculiar ways of expression, forms of dress, entertainment, etc. How far should we go in adapting the wording of the inspired biblical text to this youth subculture? Do you know of scriptural versions that do this satisfactorily? What principles are involved? What further forms of cultural translation of Scripture do youth require?

Chapter Four

Forms and Contexts of the Ministry of the Word

Outline

The principle of incarnation suggests that in breaking the bread of the Word we take advantage of the best means and situations for ministry. That means considering:

- the forms that ministry takes and the contexts where it is traditionally exercised
- the effect on these of societal and technological changes
- new approaches suggested for traditional forms of ministry.

1. Traditional forms and contexts of ministry

For Vatican II's *Dei Verbum* the ministry of the Word takes the form of "**pastoral preaching, catechesis and all Christian instruction**, in which the liturgical homily should have pride of place" (*Dei Verbum* 24). These are the means by which the bread of life is taken from the table of the Word of God, in the words of that Constitution, and offered to the faithful - or, in Pope John Paul II's words to the Biblical Commission, the means of opening up to the Christian people the springs of living water contained in the Scriptures.[1] The earliest believers were nourished in this way, according to *Acts*, even if a somewhat different nuance can be detected there: once those who received the Word were baptised, they devoted themselves to the apostles' preaching of that Word, as well as to *koinonia*, to the breaking of bread and to prayer (2.41-42), the **community context** being important.

---

[1] *AAS* 61 (1979) 607.

Breaking the bread of the Word in these contemporary forms, therefore, has **a long history**, from the early Church through the Middle Ages to the Church of Vatican II (we will need to consider the implications of these changing times and conditions). We have seen something of the thinking of great homilists and catechists of patristic times on their profession. Chrysostom, we recall, thought so highly of his preaching role as to show impatience with a congregation that could be distracted by a mere lamplighter. In more measured terms he invests that role with the dignity that comes from the Word that he as a preacher of it is serving:

> So I beg you, let us on our part imitate this [Samaritan] woman, and receive with careful attention the teachings coming from the Spirit. For what is said is not ours, nor do we utter with our own tongue whatever we say; instead, we are directed by the loving kindness of the Lord for your good and the building up of the Church of God. So do not look at my person as I say these things, dearly beloved, nor at my unworthiness; but since I am bringing what comes from the Lord, keep your attention directed to the one who sent me and so receive with earnestness what is said. Likewise in human affairs: when the Emperor, wearing his crown, dispatches letters, the bearer of them is quite likely a person of no importance... So, if such a man, who is carrying a man's letters and is bearer merely of paper, is welcomed by everyone, so much the more would you be justified in receiving with great attention the sayings sent you by the Spirit by means of us, so that you may gain a great reward for your appreciativeness.[2]

Chrysostom's simile makes clear that he sees himself bearing someone else's message, not his own. At the opening of his *Genesis* commentary he compares this Old Testament text again to letters sent by God and delivered (this time) by Moses.[3] And in the homilies on *Isaiah* 6 he develops another beautiful comparison for his preaching as a journey by sea taken by his congregation, with his own tongue as the sail, the Spirit as the breeze that fills it, and Christ as pilot.[4] No, Chrysostom is ministering God's Word

---

[2] Homily 44 on *Genesis* (*PG* 54,406).
[3] Homily 2 on *Genesis* (*PG* 53,28).
[4] Homily 'In Oziam' (*PG* 56,121).

to his congregation, **not merely sermonising**. Not all preachers have followed his example. As to his church congregation, passive attention to this Word is what is principally required, though we will see he envisages more active participation in other contexts.

St Thomas, for whom **preaching** is "officium principalissimum sacerdotis", distinguishes as some commentators do today between evangelisation and catechesis (in the sense of instruction in the rudiments of the faith, on the one hand, and preparation for the sacraments on the other), and recognised as well instruction in living the Christian life and (as part of bishops' ministry) instruction in the deepest mysteries of faith and in the perfection of the Christian life.[5] Reminiscent of that great catechist Origen, Bossuet said of preaching:

> The preachers of the Gospel ascend the pulpit in the same spirit in which they approach the altar. They ascend to celebrate a mystery, a mystery very similar to the Eucharist. For the Body of Jesus Christ is no more truly contained in the adorable sacrament than is the Truth of Jesus Christ in the preaching of the Gospel.[6]

Pius XII in *Divino Afflante Spiritu* spoke in similar terms.[7] Vatican II, as we have seen, stressed the role of the liturgical homily.[8]

"Catechesis and all Christian instruction", in that Council's words, as distinct from preaching, covers a **wide range of forms and contexts** of the ministry of the Word. St Thomas, with adults in mind, made his distinctions on the basis of progress of the believer in the life of faith; he was not thinking, as we might have until recently, rather of age differentiation, from elementary religious education of children, adolescent education, and tertiary education. Nor did St Thomas distinguish the contexts of instruction; he did not have in mind a school-based model as has predominated in Western developed countries since his time. Societal developments in centuries after him led to the **expansion**

---

[5] *Summa Theologiae* III, q.72, a.4, ad 3.
[6] Quoted by L. Claussen, "The mystery of preaching," 186.
[7] *AAS* 35 (1943) 324.
[8] Cf *Sacrosanctum Concilium* 52.

of educational opportunities generally and religious education in particular - at least for children. Advances in the theory and practice of teaching and learning improved the quality of religious education concomitantly.

The task of making the revealed Word available to the faithful has attracted generations of **scholars, translators and artists**. The arts have always served the Word well. From the stonemasons of Europe's mighty cathedrals of "the greatest of the centuries", the authors of English miracle and mystery plays, the composers of early religious music, and the Old Masters in the graphic arts, up to our own contemporary artists in various cultures, the biblical message has been reverently if unevenly conveyed to the masses - now to fall foul of the movie makers' yen for the spectacular. Versions of the Word have appeared in classical and modern languages. Scholars have not shirked the task of providing written commentaries on the Word of God. From biblical times to modern retreat movements a ministry has been practised of leading people to pray in scriptural forms and sentiments. All these artists, scholars and pastors have a role to play in ministering the Word to its intended beneficiaries. A complete listing of **contemporary forms of ministry** of the Word would also have to include radio broadcasters, TV presenters and commentators, hymn writers, cartoonists, chaplains, those engaged in ministry to the handicapped, and still others.

2. Diversity in community tradition

Practice of traditional forms of the ministry of the Word has been nuanced in the Catholic community in several ways. For the last few hundred years preaching and teaching laboured under the handicap of **depression of the Bible's importance** in Church life following the Reformation's accent on "scriptura sola". This reaction left its mark on homiletics and, in religious education more widely, on preparation of teachers, curricula and texts, all of which have until recently been markedly non-biblical.

The challenge of **bringing the Word in translation** to the people has not been met with equal enthusiasm by all Christian communities. Amongst Catholics there has at least since *Divino Afflante Spiritu* been recommendation in magisterial statement of dissemination of the Scriptures among the faithful, and *Dei Verbum* also recommends new translations. It would have to be admitted, however, that the non-Catholic Bible societies have over the years taken this responsibility much more seriously (the United Bible Societies' 1989 Scripture Language Report proudly announcing an additional 21 language editions of the Bible in 1989, bringing the total to 1928 different languages and dialects[9]); it is hard to credit today that the Knox version of the New Testament in England in 1945 and the Confraternity of Christian Doctrine New Testament in the United States in 1941 were the first Catholic translations of the Bible approved for English-speaking countries since Bishop Challoner's 1750 revision of the Rheims-Douay version of 1582-1610 - hardly a record of enthusiastic popularisation of the Word. Happily, the Catholic Biblical Federation has now joined forces with the Bible Societies in this important apostolate.

In many countries in the wake of society's accent on education, the Catholic community developed a system of elementary and secondary schools, where to some limited extent the Scriptures had a part in religious education programs. Developments in educational theory and practice affected the ministry of the Word at this level more readily than in **seminaries and other tertiary institutions** preparing prospective ministers. The result, at least for the Catholic community, has been that personal devotion to the Word could not so easily carry over to effective ministry in the manner desired by the magisterium, especially in institutions whose curricula paid scant attention to educational principles of ministry alongside study of the biblical text.

3. The influence of societal and technological developments

If the ministry of the Word in the form of "pastoral preaching, catechesis and all Christian instruction" is not proving

---

[9] Bible Society annual report, supplement to *The Sower* (1989) 6.

today as penetrating as a two-edged sword, perhaps it is because **changes in society** have undercut their effectiveness. We have seen before that the readiness of the listener in his or her own culture is critical for receptiveness, requiring sensitivity and considerateness, *synkatabasis*, on the part of the minister. Ministry of the Word today, as of any ministry to members of our society, requires acquaintance with developments in that society; our educationists tend to be sociologists, like McLuhan and Babin.

The sociologists highlight two particular societal developments that have obvious educational implications for forms and contexts of ministry. One is the change in **community structures**, affecting also communication structures. The other is the change in the process of **gathering and relaying information** and consequently of learning processes. The two changes are related, and impact upon the efficacy of ministry of the Word.

At least from the time of the Industrial Revolution and the move of people to the cities in the countries affected, there has been a **breakdown in the pattern of living** in geographical areas. Even in 1855 in addressing the British Parliament the Earl of Shaftesbury could say of England, "The parochial system is, no doubt, a beautiful thing in theory, and is of great value in small rural districts; but in the large towns it is a mere shadow and a name."[10]   Already since the availability of the printed word, there had begun the decline of tribal association (sociologists tell us) and the rise of individualism. Today, for most people in developed countries, the only meaningful communities are the family, the immediate neighbourhood, the workplace and groups where they spend leisure time (like the club and, for younger people, sporting centres and discos).

What accelerated this decline of life in community were further **changes in communications media**. The efficacy of communication of a message by spoken or written word alone, a 'hot' medium in McLuhan's terms,[11] was undercut by development of 'cool' media involving greater participation by the recipients through wider appeal to various senses. Of these

---

[10] Quoted by G. Reid, *The Gagging of God*, 23.
[11] M. McLuhan, *Understanding Media*, 31.

new media of "the electric age" by far the most influential is **television**, where the medium is the message, where concern is with effect rather than meaning, with processes rather than products, where analysis of content is almost irrelevant. The Roman poet Martial in AD 103 may have thought he had said it all in his epigram, "I won't believe it until I read it;" today he would have to recast the verse.

The effect of these societal and technological changes on religious practice has been profound, for some traditions more than others. Reformist communities in being predominantly biblical ran the risk of becoming a literary subculture in a modern world where people were largely non-literary. An alternative response, visible in the Catholic community, was for people to move to adopt a more liturgical, more devotional, less biblical form of Christianity. Modern man and woman are in their busy work-a-day lives receiving their information and education through popular newspapers, slick advertising, TV or VTR (videotape recorder); they rarely read a book or listen to a sermon. Preaching the Word to serried ranks of a large, impassive congregation in a barn-like building could not hold the fascination of cooler forms of communication. The great preachers of former days, like Fulton Sheen, would look melodramatic by comparison with TV's preference for the softsell; McLuhan speaks of "the death of all the salesmen at one stroke of the TV axe."[12]   To remain effective, this form of **ministry would have to adjust**.

To highlight the adjustment this involves for the ministry of the Word, Gavin Reid in *The Gagging of God. The Failure of the Church to Communicate in the Television Age* reports an (imaginary) interview with the principal of a theological college.

> "Good afternoon," we say as we settle down in his study overlooking the lovely grounds that surround the training college. "What do you consider your job to be?"
> "Well, that's quite easy to answer," he replies. "My job, under God, is to prepare men for effective ministry in the years ahead."

---

[12] *Ibid.*, 36.

"I see," we reply. "What do you consider to be the tasks of a minister in the Church?"

"Well, of course, first and foremost to be a preacher of the gospel. In addition to that, however, he must be able to shepherd the congregation and teach them so that they are equipped to go out into daily life and witness for Christ."

"How do you prepare them for this preaching and teaching?"

"In two ways, really," he replies. "Firstly by the academic study of the Bible and theology. Secondly by practical lectures such as homiletics and pastoralia where we teach them how to preach and how to carry out the routine procedures of a minister."

"You say that you teach the students how to preach. What in fact do you do?"

"Well, they are taught how to analyse a passage of scripture. This is very important because we believe that preaching is not about the opinions of men but about the word of God. Then we show how the passage can be broken down for sermon presentation and we discuss how to illustrate points."

"You say illustrate - do you mean visual aids?"

"Oh no!" He chuckles at our ignorance. "No - I mean by the use of anecdote and drawing examples and parallels from everyday experience."

"Do you, in fact, do anything about visual aids?"

"Not really. But we do have a member of staff who is a bit of a dab hand at children's talks and he sometimes gives an end-of-term lecture on preparing visual aids."

"That's for children's talks?"

"Of course."[13]

Reid concludes by wondering if the college in question was preparing ministers or antiquarians. Effective ministry rests on **employment of the media available** in any age for good communication.

The **positive advantages of modern media** for teaching and learning (which we shall examine specifically in Chapter 8) are that they encourage total involvement and participation. While preachers could ignore this truth without immediate reaction, and likewise to an extent seminary professors and college lecturers, children of the electric age forced educationists

---

[13] *The Gagging of God*, 40-41.

at another level to respond to it, so that the new audiovisual media have been exploited in classrooms everywhere. Religious education (RE) in this less academic form has also had to respond to philosophical scrutiny and debate as well as to these social and technological changes.

For instance, the **ideal locus of RE** - whether school, parish, home - has been re-examined, and magisterial statement in documents like *Catechesi Tradendae* has come down in favour of those smaller, more intimate, meaningful situations spoken of before for catechesis in the sense of faith-sharing; less confidential, even less participative situations like lecture halls and classrooms may suffice for more academic education. The **scope of RE** has also been re-examined to highlight the neglect of adults' faith development in countries where resources have been directed mainly to schools and other educational contexts for children only; the education of adults in the faith has become a priority, along with programs to initiate adults into the Christian community, like RCIA (see Appendix Two). **Teacher preparation for RE** has had to become more professional, particularly since decrease in the number of religious available from those institutes originally founded to cope with the greater accent on schooling in the 18th and 19th centuries. Such professional development for the ministry of the Word has probably affected least of all the preacher of the Word.

4. Different approaches to traditional forms of ministry

Well before the social and educational developments and media inventions that have drastically influenced the efficacy of the various forms of the ministry of the Word, even as convinced a preacher as Chrysostom realised that he in his pulpit had no monopoly on the action of the Spirit where the text of Scripture was concerned. He could envisage **other contexts and other processes** by which the inspired Word could touch believers. He tells his congregation:

> If we look on things aright, we will be able while at home,
> before dining or after dining, by taking the sacred Books in
> hand, to gain benefit from them and provide spiritual
> nourishment for our soul... This is our salvation, this is
> spiritual treasure, this is security. If we thus strengthen
> ourselves each day - by reading, by listening, by spiritual
> discourse - we will be able to remain unconquered, and render
> the snares of the devil ineffectual, and reach the kingdom of
> heaven.[14]

Chrysostom as preacher in Antioch certainly expected his
congregation to attend fully to his commentary on biblical texts
(no mere sermonising for him); but he could appreciate that **the
family circle** might also be a congenial situation for breaking the
bread of the Word. Elsewhere he admits that even in other
situations the process might continue:

> On your part, keep in mind what we've been saying,
> remember it, teach it to those who did not hear it, and let each
> of you ponder it, whether in church, in the street, or at home.
> Nothing, you know, is more delightful than listening to God's
> Word.[15]

For Chrysostom "reading, listening and spiritual discourse"
were forms of receiving or transmitting the Word under the
influence of the Spirit along with his own homilies. The contexts
he envisages admitted of an intimacy that was probably true also
of situations of ministry mentioned in the New Testament, unlike
the modern preaching of the Word to large congregations of
people arrayed geometrically in parallel rows - a situation not
conducive to **intimacy and participation**. We have seen *Acts* 2.42
speaking of the apostles' teaching and *koinonia* together; the
context and process are important if communication is to take
place.

Since New Testament and patristic times those societal
changes and educational developments have occurred that
further recommend attention to context and process as well as to

---

[14] Homily 10 on *Genesis* (PG 53,90).
[15] Sermon 8 on *Genesis* (PG 54,619).

the forms of the ministry of the Word. Learning theories have stressed **dialogue and interaction** along with direct instruction. The small group, tutorial, seminar have grown up alongside, if not actually replaced, the mass lecture, especially in adult education. The immediacy, participation, in-depth treatment of topics made possible by the cool medium of television and video have been adopted in religious education. Settings have been chosen that allow for the recreation of a sense of community and the intercommunication that goes with it - family, neighbourhood, leisure in-groups. Attention to content comes after **choice of setting, context, and structure**. This principle was accepted by the bishops at the 1987 Synod on the laity:

> Many parishes, whether established in regions affected by urban progress or in missionary territory, cannot do their work effectively because they lack material resources or ordained men or are too big geographically or because of the particular circumstances of some Christians (e.g., exiles or migrants). So that all parishes of this kind may be truly communities of Christians, local ecclesial authorities ought to foster the following: a) adaptation of parish structures according to the full flexibility granted by canon law, especially in promoting participation by the lay faithful in pastoral responsibilities;   b) small, basic or so-called 'living' communities, where the faithful can communicate the Word of God and express it in service and love to one another; these communities are true expressions of ecclesial communion and centres of evangelisation, in communion with their pastors. (Proposition 11)[16]

As we have noted, **preaching the Word** has yet to be fully influenced by these developments, probably because curricula in institutions preparing teachers have been proof against them. There have been those like A. Nebreda who have expressed the unease felt in East and West about a style of preaching that accentuated biblical content without attention to the needs of the listeners; but in suggesting (in *Kerygma in Crisis?*) a solution dealing with content alone, recommending a dose of apologetics along with the kerygmatic approach, he continued to ignore the

---

[16] Quoted by Pope John Paul II in *Christifideles Laici*, Rome: Vatican, 1989, #26.

medium as message and say nothing of context and setting. Others like Ellul have simply decried the decline of the spoken word before the inroads of images: "The present humiliation of the word is only the current version of a permanent reality: people detest the fundamental word, which nevertheless establishes them as *human* beings."[17]

With the realisation that previous approaches to preaching the Word had been less efficacious with those who attended, let alone those absenting themselves in vast numbers, preachers in countries like Scotland, Germany and France **experimented** with radio broadcasting, paper-back sermons, dialogue preaching, records of famous preachers, and made a study of the successes of Black preaching in the United States.[18]   Beginning with *Ezekiel* 3.15, "I came to the exiles at Telabib, who dwelt by the river Chebar. For seven days I sat where they sat," H. M. Mitchell offers "an analysis of the genius of **Black preaching**" in terms of preaching as Folk Culture, as Meaningful Personal Presence, as Celebration, as Biblical Storytelling, as Folk Language, as Dialogue.[19] There can be no doubt that this approach to preaching encourages lively interchange, participation, involvement. In any case, sitting where the listeners sit is an instructive experience for any speaker, whether preacher, lecturer, teacher, parent.

Communities for whom preaching the Word in church has always had high priority and forms the focus of the weekly assembly have had to face the question (after conclusive proof of diminishing effect), "Should we scrap sermons?" Some have conceded that the old monologue-lecture style sermon/homily could have some effect if improved with the use of aids promoting involvement like blackboards, overhead projectors, notebooks and pencils. A team of presenters could be used after discussion of the best means of involvement. Films, videos, filmstrips, slides, tapes could be used for part of the weekly hour. Splitting up the congregation into smaller groups for discussion of the topic is

---

[17] *La parole humiliée*, Paris: Editions du Seuil, 1981, 195.
[18] Cf D. W. Cleverley Ford, *The Ministry of the Word*, London: Hodder and Stoughton, 1979, 85-86.
[19] *The Recovery of Preaching*.

another alternative. More adventurous is the use of drama-mime and dance drama.[20] Much of this **re-thinking of structures** springs from dissatisfaction with the typical church building as a setting for the ministry of the Word today, leading to the search for alternative settings and ultimately design of more suitable buildings. In short, if traditional forms of ministering the Word are to be effective for today's recipients accustomed to different social habits and enjoying sophisticated means of instruction, **new approaches** to that ministry are called for.

The Incarnation as the supreme example of *koinonia* and as paradigm for the scriptural Word requires of us the continual reassessment of forms of ministry of the Word. "Remember not the former things, nor consider the things of old," says the Lord, the Creator. "Behold, I am doing a new thing; now it springs forth, do you not perceive it?" (Is 43.18-19). If the Word of God speaks of continuing innovation, the ministry of that Word - "Pastoral preaching, catechesis and all Christian instruction" - must be alert to **recognise and adapt to changing conditions** and possibilities; considering only "the things of old" (even if important for people to hear) is an unworthy service. Jesus himself warns against the harm that comes from trying to contain the novelty of his message within old forms and practices - new wine in old wineskins (Lk 5.37). His ministers should ensure that the potency of the message is not impaired by an outdated medium.

Bibliography

E. Achtemeier, *Creative Preaching,* Nashville: Abingdon, 1980

L. Claussen, "The mystery of preaching: *Christus praedicat Christum*" in K. Rahner et al, *The Word. Readings in Theology,* New York: Kenedy, 1964, 186-95

R. H. Fuller, *The Use of the Bible in Preaching,* Philadelphia: Fortress, 1981

---

[20] G. Reid, *The Gagging of God,* 102-103.

M. McLuhan, *Understanding Media. The Extensions of Man*, London: Sphere Books, 1967

F. McNulty (ed.), *Preaching Better*, New York: Paulist, 1985

D. E. Miller, *Story and Context. An Introduction to Christian Education*, Nashville: Abingdon, 1987

H. M. Mitchell, *The Recovery of Preaching*, London: Hodder and Stoughton, 1979

A. M. Nebreda, *Kerygma in Crisis?*, Manila: East Asian Pastoral Institute, 1971

E. A. Nida, *Message and Mission. The Communication of the Christian Faith*, New York: Harper and Row, 1960

P. Palmer, *The Lively Audience. A Study of Children Around the TV Set*, Sydney: Allen and Unwin, 1986

G. Reid, *The Gagging of God. The Failure of the Church to Communicate in the Television Age*, London: Hodder and Stoughton, 1969

relevant journals: *Church*
                     Diakonia (Mainz)
                     Esprit et Vie
                     The Furrow
                     Homiletic and Pastoral Review
                     Priest
                     United Bible Societies Bulletin
                     Word in Life
                     Worship

Practical exercises for ministry

1. In which form of the ministry of the Word are you (principally) engaged (possibly several)? Perhaps you have noticed changes in its exercise over time in response to social and educational developments; list these. Would you say that in regard to approaches, contexts, educational media it is adapted to people's needs and expectations today? What remains to be done to achieve this?

2. In your experience, is the liturgical homily as influential a form of ministry of the Word as Vatican II expects it to be (see *Dei Verbum* 24, *Sacrosanctum Concilium* 24,35,52)? If not, what could be done to make it more efficacious? What can we do as listeners to the Word to benefit more fully from this ministry?

3. Some may say the Scriptures are written by adults for adults; would you agree? Have we really profited sufficiently from educational developments to bring young people into touch with the Word, especially in the Catholic community? Or, if you believe we should concentrate on adult biblical formation, what is in fact being done for them? Perhaps we can learn from other communities.

4. Read again the imaginary interview by Gavin Reid in this chapter with the principal of an institution preparing people for ministry of the Word. How adequate do you find the principal's approach to his task? In detail, what needs to be included in the curriculum of such institutions to ensure adequate preparation for that ministry in its various forms today? (Include practical work in your curriculum design.)

Chapter Five

Planning for a ministry of the Word

Outline

An effective ministry of the Word that achieves true *koinonia* does not occur by chance. It requires remote and proximate planning appropriate to each form of ministry, including

- consideration of Word and listener
- basic rationale and educational goals of ministry
- provision for particular experiences and outcomes in the listener.

1. Purpose and design in the gift of the Word

The purpose of the biblical *koinonia*, as of the historical Incarnation, is a relationship between the participants in this fellowship, between the listener to the Word and him who "has spoken through the prophets." The ministry of the Word exists to promote and facilitate this relationship, by introducing the listener to the spoken Word and by providing for a growing familiarity. The economy of incarnation suggests that **the relationship will not develop by accident**, magic, good fortune, just as the divine initiative did not occur through any such factor. The author of *Ephesians*, for instance, repeatedly accentuates the choice, will, purpose, plan responsible for bringing us so many blessings (the beautiful sense of the Pauline 'mystery of Christ'):

> Blessed be the God and Father of our Lord Jesus Christ, who has blessed us in Christ with every spiritual blessing in the heavenly places, even as he *chose* us in him before the foundation of the world, that we should be holy and blameless before him. He *destined* us in love to be his sons through Jesus Christ, according to the *purpose* of his *will*, to the praise of his glorious grace which he freely bestowed on us in the Beloved. In him we have redemption through his

blood, the forgiveness of our trespasses, according to the riches of his grace which he lavished upon us. For he has made known to us in all wisdom and insight the mystery of his *will*, according to his *purpose* which he set forth in Christ as a *plan* for the fulness of time (1.3-10).

The ministry of the Word, likewise, involves deliberation and assiduity if it is to succeed in its goal of promoting the relationship between Word and believer. We are fortunate to be living in a time when the Church acknowledges the irreplaceable role of the bread of the Word in nourishing the faithful (cf Vatican II, *Dei Verbum* 21) and the concomitant need for adequate preparation of ministers for breaking that bread. What remains is for those ministers, suitably prepared, to apply themselves professionally to **the demanding task of planning** for a fruitful ministry.

Previous chapters have outlined what calls for **remote consideration** when doing this planning. There is, firstly, the nature and purpose of the Word, incarnate in the Scriptures, which suggests an urgency and at the same time imposes conditions arising out of the intentions and situation of its ancient oriental authors in terms of accessibility of its message. Can this message be translated directly (the minister would need to consider) into all situations and for all listeners irrespective of historical and cultural differences? Then there is the condition of the recipient, the listener, believer or non-believer, with all the factors of age, sex, human and religious development, cultural conditioning - in short, readiness for the Word - that we have outlined in Chapters Two and Three, prompting Augustine's criterion for effective ministry, *pro capacitate ac viribus audientis*: "with respect for the listener's capacity and resources." Thirdly, planning will need to take account of the possibilities for ministry of appropriate forms, contexts, structures and approaches in the light of educational advances and developments in society and technology.

2. A rationale for ministry

Weighing these fundamental considerations, the minister of the Word can proceed to plan for effective communication and response. Not, however, immediately at the level of content, method, strategies and materials. There is first the question of rationale, justification, basic values and assumptions, **broad aims and educational goals**. These may be implicit in my zeal to communicate the biblical message to my congregation, group or class; but I would do well to lay them out clearly before proceeding to plan further for particular objectives or outcomes. Otherwise, later in evaluating the success of my ministry I may find that the enjoyment I had in the process of communicating God's Word was not matched by the effect of my efforts on my listeners, who were uninterested or bewildered, disturbed or offended by what I had to offer them irrespective of their needs and receptiveness. We have to plan for an interchange between us and our listeners - or, rather, between the Word and his listeners - such that they will respond in faith, hope and love. That was Augustine's general plan in his ministry of the Word to beginners outlined in *D e Catechizandis Rudibus*:

> Whatever you say, say it in such a way that on hearing it your listeners may come to believe, by believing may come to hope, and by hoping may come to love.[1]

(The Fathers of Vatican II thought it worthwhile to invoke this principle in opening their Constitution on the Word.)

We have seen these great patristic catechists and homilists raising with themselves questions such as the following before entering upon their ministry; we would do well to consider them ourselves. Why am I, after my professional studies of the text of the Bible and (hopefully) my professional preparation as an educator, now entering upon this course of biblical education with this school class or this adult group, this church congregation or these seminary students, with this individual or prayer group? It could be for **any number of reasons**, all well-motivated but some less educationally sound than others and less likely to promote that relationship that is the purpose of biblical *koinonia*.

---

[1] 4,8 (*PL* 40,316).

My basic motivation might, for instance, be nothing more substantial than **a passing fad,** a hunch that a biblically-based RE program is the done thing these days at whatever level of schooling, after many lean years when the Bible was never to be found in classrooms, before Jungmann[2] and Hofinger[3] rediscovered it and launched the kerygmatic method. A teacher's excitement, however, over a long lost and recently discovered resource in his or her own life does not always make for good teaching with others not feeling this sense of loss and discovery; we saw educationists like Loukes and Goldman[4] reporting on the indifferent success of scriptural education in English (state-run) schools, and experience taught Catholic teachers as well that unlimited doses of Bible do not overly impress young people of school age.

Another praiseworthy, if educationally inadequate, reason for implementing a program of scriptural education might be that **swing of the pendulum in the Church** generally, that the Church has moved from centuries of practical discouragement of biblical studies to open encouragement; so the diet of all Christians of whatever age in whatever situation should become equally scriptural as eucharistic. That is surely a move in the right direction in the wake of *Divino Afflante Spiritu* and *Dei Verbum,* correcting the post-Reformation imbalance. The trouble is that the new diet could prove indigestible if offered indiscriminately to all; Coheleth could remind us there are times and seasons for breaking the bread of the Word efficaciously. Scripture ought perhaps become the soul of theology for seminarians,[5] but that is not necessarily a recipe for all educational endeavour.

Another reason that sometimes leads in high schools to the adoption of a biblical studies program is that it is **a safe, non-confessional study** that can be followed irrespective of the stage of

[2] *Die Frohbotschaft und Unsere Glaubensverkündigung,* Regensburg: Pustet, 1936 (ET *The Good News Yesterday and Today,* New York: Sadlier, 1962).

[3] *Katechetik Heute,* Freiburg: Herder, 1961 (ET *Teaching All Nations,* Freiburg: Herder, 1961).

[4] *Readiness for Religion. A Basis for Developmental Religious Education,* London: Routledge and Kegan Paul, 1965.

[5] Cf Vatican II, Decree on Priestly Formation 16, quoting Leo XIII, *Providentissimus Deus, AAS* 26 (1893-94) 283.

faith development of students. The emphasis in such a program falls on imparting and absorbing information about texts, authors, historical and social contexts. A Bible as Literature program can likewise be conducted without presuming a faith dimension to the study. Whether such acquaintance with the Scriptures promotes the *koinonia* of the scriptural incarnation is doubtful, but the non-confessional approach is 'safe' enough for it to be approved by state education departments; that can be sufficient justification for some teachers.

An adequate reason for breaking the bread of the Word with many groups of Catholic adults is their **sense of neglect of the Bible,** of loss, of deprivation, of hunger arising from an upbringing in a non-biblical age. Their home never knew a Bible, except perhaps as a register of births, deaths and marriages, their classrooms and teachers were likewise innocent of any Bible. Raised on a Latin liturgy and (at best) Bible history, they are physically incapable of finding their way around the Bible just as they are ignorant also of its theological themes. They thrill to the discovery of the multiple voices and layers and meanings of the inspired writings, and long to plumb the depths of this 'Protestant' book. Helping them make this acquaintance is an enriching exercise of the ministry of the Word for all concerned, a truly educational experience in Augustine's sense. The proviso, of course, is that these adults (not children, generally) have this sense of loss, this yen - not just the minister.

My rationale for bringing young people and older to the Scriptures - in some appropriate context and at some appropriate stage - might be somewhat different again: to **put them in touch with Christian tradition** in a way and form that differs from liturgical tradition and doctrinal tradition. They celebrate the Christian Passover, they listen to their guides and teachers, they share in the community's lived experience; but in scriptural tradition they find another way of entering the Christian mystery, of sharing in the experience of God's action (pre-eminently but not solely in Jesus) that constituted the community, that reveals who their God is and how they are related to him, that evokes their faith in him which they express and which commits them to him.

That is no mere passing fad, but an adequate rationale for introducing people to the Scriptures and fostering their acquaintance with them. Deciding how much when, of course, requires further educational judgements; but at least our values and overall goals in such a ministry are sound.

3. Planning for experiences and outcomes

If we are convinced that our reasons for ministering the Word to this or that group are not only above reproach but also educationally sound, and if we are taking into account as well those three basic considerations - the Word itself, the condition of the listener, appropriate forms and contexts of ministry - then we can conduct our planning further. What can we achieve with these people? How can they experience a meeting with the Word of God?

Each of these questions framed by ministers of the Word in their planning for ministry expresses the ultimate aim of enabling the believer to participate in the divine *koinonia* of the Scriptures. Yet each represents a rather different approach to the educational task, which may suit one form of ministry rather than another - teaching a small group of advanced students, for instance, rather than preaching to a large congregation. In the former case we may have particular **objectives or outcomes** for the semester's work (e.g., knowledge of Jeremiah's prophetic message in the context of the Judah of the years before the Exile), which an overall program expects the students to achieve and which will be assessed in due course. For the preacher to his Holy Week congregation it is their experience of Psalm 22, with its echoes of the Lord's Passion at that particular season, that he hopes will sink deep and remain with them, without his being able to guarantee the **depth of experience or response**. Chrysostom with his congregation, systematic commentator though he was, realised that spiritual influence came also from another source:

> As I was saying, then, our hall is full - or, if you like, the tossing sea is everywhere calm, the tempestuous ocean is quite steady. Come, let us launch the boat, loosing our tongue

> in place of the sail, trimming our canvas to the grace of the
> Spirit instead of the breeze, employing for pilot the Cross
> instead of rudder and oar.[6]

Both situations, classroom and church, call for planning if the ministry is to be effective, even if accent seems to fall on outcomes in one case and on experience or process in the other. Educationists and psychologists in speaking of **educational objectives or outcomes** list various kinds: knowledge and understandings, attitudes and values, skills of different types; they have also been classified as cognitive, affective, and psychomotor objectives respectively. All are relevant to the ministry of the Word in one form or another; and since what is at stake is that share in scriptural *koinonia*, we should heed educationists' call for precision as to our objectives in ministry, while remembering the reminder of others that not all outcomes are so easily identifiable.[7]

For it is possible to be unclear or unrealistic about the outcomes of our ministry, though this can be avoided by planning. At the level of mere knowledge, we can plan for thorough grasp of a text's meaning by close exegesis in working with a skilled tertiary group of student. It may be, on the contrary, that a concentrated study of *Ezekiel* is not what this group is ready for just now. We may, in fact, think it is important to **provide beginners with basic information** about the structure of the Bible, names of books and biblical characters. This would involve not only elementary understanding but also the physical skill of handling the Bible and flipping it open at, say, *Nehemiah* or *Nahum* at call so as to dispel that affective disability so often found in Catholics when confronted with the Bible of feeling utterly lost, especially as regards the Old Testament. We may even have to practise them in the basics of acquiring a Bible, choosing a good translation, becoming accustomed to carrying it and holding it - modest objectives indeed. No use presuming the group or person is capable of exhaustive exegesis when they are still at the

---

[6] Homily 4 'In Oziam' (*PG* 56,121).
[7] Cf L. Brady, *Curriculum Development*, 61-63.

discovery stage; Catholics are generally coming from along way back where familiarity with the Bible is concerned.

In another case it may be thought appropriate to **develop people's biblical culture** for the sake of their general education. Educated Christians should know something of the book behind this Religion of the Book, something of the biblical world and its characters that have inspired the world's literatures. Reading Milton's *Paradise Lost* or Patrick White's *The Tree of Man* without some knowledge of *Genesis* would be an unnecessary handicap. Our cultural horizons should accommodate the great moral and dogmatic figures of Scripture, like Esther and Job, Barnabas and Judith. As Chrysostom told his congregation, "If you want to talk about a king, there is a king in these stories; if it's about soldiers, or family matters, or public affairs, you will see a great abundance of these examples in the Scriptures."[8] The great homilist thought this *an* acceptable objective in his preaching - though he went beyond that, could even flatter his audience with the ability to choose between variant interpretations of a text, and certainly had at heart their moral and spiritual progress. In fact, to be consistent, we should also on this reasoning introduce our listeners to the Koran and the Vedas. So, if this is an educational objective in our ministry, it is a limited one.

Beyond these limited aims of providing basic biblical information and depthing our listeners' religious culture, our objective might extend to **helping them meet Jesus** in the pages of the New Testament. They meet him in other ways, of course - at prayer, in the Eucharist, in their daily life and dealings with others; but the biblical encounter is special, and adults and children need to be introduced to him there. Much thought has been given in drawing up religious education programs as to the best age to concentrate on this meeting with Jesus (to the exclusion of Old Testament material), and we can be guided in this decision. It should be a prayerful encounter rather than simply reading stories of Jesus, if a meeting is to occur. Such an objective, of course, comes close to the purpose of *koinonia*, though it is still limited:

---

[8] Homily 1 on David and Saul (*PG* 54,686).

keeping the focus on Jesus runs the risk of missing out on the mystery of Christ as a whole.

Related to this objective of meeting Jesus in the text of the Gospels is another in our ministry: **reading and listening to the Word of God**. Reverence for the Word does not come naturally to Catholics in the West, to judge from many of our liturgies. Compare the respect accorded to the Word of God in Eastern liturgies, where the Scriptures beautifully bound are borne aloft, incensed and enthroned as the Word of God enfleshed in language and literature, as *Dei Verbum* is now reminding us at the behest of the Greek Fathers like Chrysostom:

> Be sure to give all your attention; for the reading of the Scriptures is an opening of the heavens.[9]

> The mouths of the inspired authors are the mouth of God; such a mouth would say nothing idle. Accordingly, let there be nothing idle in our attention.[10]

To recognise and reverence the Word of God in the text of the Bible is an experience that should become habitual for Christians, like their reverence for the Eucharist; it is a continuing objective of the ministry of the Word, and educational judgement will suggest to us appropriate times, ages and occasions. Failure to provide these opportunities has been a terrible deprivation for the Catholic community in particular over a long period, one that our ministry must remedy.

We have suggested that meeting Jesus in the New Testament - praiseworthy objective though it is - could fall short of Paul's thinking about our **acquaintance with the total mystery of Christ**, the entire plan of salvation that the Bible as a whole presents. Catholics generally have not been much exposed to the Old Testament outside of those rather inconsequentially selected passages at Sunday Mass, and they are unsure of their way around it; teachers hesitate to program for it, being diffident themselves, and young people thus have to settle for the New

---

[9] Homily 2 'In Oziam' (*PG* 56,109).
[10] *Ibid*. (*PG* 56,110).

Testament. Dispelling the ignorance of Christ that ensues from this unfamiliarity with the whole Bible (in Jerome's words)[11] is another urgent objective for the ministry of the Word, involving an accent on the overall pattern and theological message of Torah, Prophets and Writings, in the manner of Jesus' lectures on hermeneutics at *Luke* 24 and *John* 5, in addition to familiarity with the New Testament. Fortunately, the liturgy at Easter reinforces our pedagogy here by leading us through texts illustrating the history of salvation so that we may appreciate the significance of Jesus' Paschal Mystery by contextualising it.

From the point of view of the *koinonia* that the Scriptures represent, **the most urgent objective** of the ministry of the Word must be to achieve the ideal that Vatican II enunciates of the place of the Scriptures in the life of the faithful:

> The Church has always venerated the divine Scriptures just as she has the very body of the Lord, since especially in the sacred liturgy she does not cease to take the bread of life from the table of both the Word of God and the Body of Christ, and offer it to the faithful.

By introducing people young and old to the scriptural Word in various ways (*pro capacitate ac viribus audientis*, in Augustine's phrase: to the extent of the listener's capacity and resources) we are ensuring that their **spiritual diet** is a balanced diet, that they are not being deprived of the bread of life, that (in the words of John Paul II to the Pontifical Biblical Commission)[12] the spring of living water is being opened up to them. For too long the spirituality of Catholic people was unbalanced because this bread and this living water were not readily available. The ministry of the Word can adjust this imbalance by helping people's style of prayer, theologising, educational planning and teaching to become more scriptural. That is no modest objective, of course. It calls for careful planning and involves a range of meaningful personal experiences that perhaps exceed assessable outcomes; *Luke* 24 does not speak of Jesus evaluating his lecture on hermeneutics to the disciples on the way to Emmaus, yet they knew their hearts had

---

[11] Commentary on *Isaiah*, prol. (*PL* 24,17).
[12] *AAS* 61 (1979) 607.

burned within them as he explained the Scriptures. Vatican II envisages all Christians having this heart-warming experience.

There are many **other objectives and experiences** that could be enunciated for the ministry of the Word, always taking into account the nature of the Word and the condition of its recipients. People are forever seeking light on a range of faith concerns, from age-old problems of evil and suffering to the worries of the nuclear age, and we can endeavour to bring the Scriptures to bear sensitively on these concerns. It may be that we have to speak or write for an audience unknown to us on broadly scriptural topics; our impact here will be less predictable. And so on.

4. From objectives to teaching processes

If our ministry is to be effective in these many situations of need, **planning is required**, from the moment of conviction that the Word can speak to this particular group or this particular person up to the process of communication in preaching or teaching, prayer or counselling, or some other form of ministry. The success of a sermon or retreat will depend much on the force and prayerfulness of the experience we devise for the group or congregation, under the limitations of setting and available resources. (There is also the proviso that we have seen Chrysostom making, namely, that in biblical *koinonia* we are mere facilitators of a relationship that stems ultimately from the action of the Spirit. **We cannot manipulate that influence** - merely plan for it, and should certainly not undermine it by slipshod planning.)

In the case of **a sustained teaching program**, we need to be clear about our rationale and broad educational goals, and precise also about the particular outcomes we hope to achieve in our listeners. Our course design, or curriculum, will in these cases reach to the general teaching strategies we judge likely to produce these instructional objectives. The sequence or course itself will then be planned in terms of distinct units of biblical material appropriate for particular occasions - the content of our sessions, details of which we will consider in Chapter 6. Success with these sessions would also call for attention to particular objectives and particular teaching strategies, materials, aids. At the conclusion of the course or series of sessions (and at times throughout it), we would do well to evaluate the success of our ministry by matching the actual outcomes against those we planned to achieve; adjustment could then be made in future. Obviously this kind of planning is not suited to every form of the ministry of the Word. Teaching the Scriptures could benefit from it, and so we might look at its stages in diagram form:

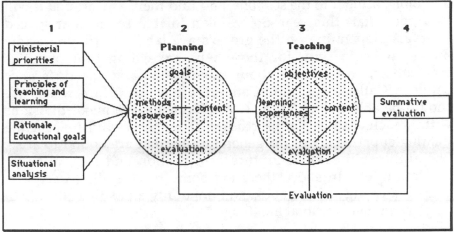

FLOWCHART SHOWING STAGES OF PLANNING[13]

Let us illustrate these planning stages with **an example**. We have been invited to work in a parish situation with a group of Catholic parents anxious to "learn (more) about the Bible". That seems an eminently desirable focus for our ministry, especially as these parents are themselves engaged in voluntary work for the CCD (Confraternity of Christian Doctrine), instructing young Catholics in state schools; so we accept the invitation. On meeting them for the first time (in a small hall with comfortable chairs and an overhead projector), when almost none of them come equipped with a Bible, we find they are new to Bible study apart from some exposure to the Gospels at school (many years back); so we can

---

[13] Cf Posner and Rudnitsky, *Course Design*, 9, 12; J. Hawes, "Models and muddles in school-based curriculum development," *The Leader* 1 (1979) 24; M. Flynn, *The Effectiveness of Catholic Schools*, Sydney: St Paul Publications, 1985, 118.

presume nothing and must proceed at a slow pace. Yet they are regular Mass-goers. We agree they should "learn (more) about the Bible", if only to ensure that their spiritual life should become as scriptural as it is eucharistic, and that they should thus participate more fully in the *koinonia* God has offered them in the Incarnation (**Stage 1** in flowchart above).

We perceive it is much too early to do close textual study with the group; getting them to acquire a (suitable translation of the) Bible, bring it to the sessions, and find their way around it will be a good start this year. So we plan for ten sessions at spaced intervals, depending on the group's availability, bringing a few Bibles to begin with for those who take longer to organise themselves, and talking about translations and the difference between Catholic and non-Catholic Bibles; in future weeks we should be able to look at the two testaments, the major divisions within each, and a sample reading from these divisions, while treating superficially of the general topics that are bound to arise, like authorship of the Scriptures, inspiration and biblical truth, revelation, etc. In short, there are some basic skills to acquire, some knowledge of this book, and hopefully a positive attitude to its place in their spiritual life (**Stage 2**).

Each week we set ourselves the target of increasing overall familiarity with the Bible. We continue insisting all participants bring their Bible (once acquired) to every session, and we keep them handling it, opening it at the major divisions of Old and New Testaments, finally feeling comfortable in turning up individual books without reference to Table of Contents or tabs down the side. Questions are encouraged at every stage, and participants urged to challenge every obscurity in our presentation. Handling and reading the biblical text is basic. No written work is involved apart from note-taking by those inclined. We also read and pray together one psalm a week to keep a spiritual character to sessions that could otherwise be pedestrian. We make each person's Bible the basic resource, while developing a wider view through overhead transparencies showing the general structure of the Bible, the major divisions, particular books, and also brief summaries of those general topics that arise (authorship, e.g.).

Colourful materials from the Bible Societies, such as psalm leaflets, also help (**Stage 3**).

Occasionally during the ten week period we monitor progress and assess people's success in acquiring basic skills (such as by having a speed test of finding the speaker in a dozen nominated verses from the Bible, by a simulation game, etc.). At the end of the ten weeks, while an examination is not appropriate for this group of beginners, we do the evaluation more formally by discussing or even asking for a written report of what the participants feel they have acquired through the course, and we match this with the outcomes we planned for. We consider whether the exercise has been worthwhile, and plan next time perhaps to take things at a different speed, change the venue, select a more appropriate hour, etc. (**Stage 4**).

5. Conclusion

This accent on planning for our involvement in so elevated an endeavour as the ministry of the Word may seem contrived, even mechanical; educationists also have their reservations about an objectives curriculum model, and we have seen that other approaches suit different forms of ministry. Yet we should recall again the fact of incarnation and the **reliance on human resources** and processes that this involves. What we have to offer as ministers beyond enthusiasm is our intellect and ability to learn from others' findings and our mistakes - hence the dependence in this and other chapters of this book on the work of psychologists and educationists as much as on biblical scholars and magisterial directives. To fly in the face of such incarnational factors would be unwise; as Chrysostom advised his simple hearers long ago,

> What is the use of proving God's immunity from suffering to the person who doesn't believe he exercises any providence, or cares for things that exist, or even exists himself? So first of all talk to them about these things.[14]

---

[14] Homily on *Psalm VI* (PG 55,71).

If attention to such details in embarking on ministry seems pedestrian, remember that what is at stake is no trifle: it is nothing less than **relationship with the Father** through his revealed Word - *koinonia* in biblical terms. Breaking the bread of that Word with a view to that relationship cannot be too painstaking.

Part Two will address some of the factors to be considered in planning for the particular ministry of *teaching* the Word.

Bibliography

J. M. Atkin, "Behavioural objectives in curriculum design: a cautionary note" in B. R. Worthen, J. R. Sanders, *Educational Evaluation: Theory and Practice*, Belmont: Wadsworth, 1973, 232-39

M. Boys, "Studying and teaching the Scriptures with imagination," *Word in Life* 38 (November 1990) 10-13

L. Brady, *Curriculum Development*, Sydney: Prentice Hall, 1990, 3rd ed.

N. L. Gage, D.C. Berliner, *Educational Psychology*, Dallas: Houghton Mifflin, 1984, 3rd ed.

R. M.Gagné, L. J. Briggs, *Principles of Instructional Design*, New York: Holt, Rinehart and Winston, 1979

R. C. Hill, "A biblically-based RE: why?", *Word in Life* 37 (1989 May) 9-12

W. B. Kolesnik, *Learning: Educational Applications*, Boston: Allyn and Bacon, 1976

G. R. Lefrancois, *Psychology for Teaching*, Belmont: Wadsworth, 1985, 5th ed.

S. Owen, S. Parker Blount, H. Moscow, *Educational Psychology. An Introduction*, Boston: Little, Brown & Co, 1978

G. J. Posner, A. N. Rudnitsky, *Course Design. A Guide to Curriculum Development for Teachers*, New York-London: Longman, 1982, 2nd ed.

P. J. Stuhlmiller, "Basic goals for biblical education," *PACE* 10 (1979)

relevant journals: *Educational Theory*
Harvard Educational Review
Journal of Research and Development in Education
Review of Educational Research
Teachers College Record
Teaching and Teacher Education

Practical exercises for ministry

1. Recall your most recent exercise of the ministry of the Word (e.g., a sermon, class, retreat). How successful would you rate it? To what extent did this degree of success depend on your amount of planning? Retrace the process of planning and implementation you followed. Would you do it differently next time?

2. You have been asked to help with the parish retreat, taking responsibility for half a dozen biblical meditations for adults. Outline your planning for these sessions with this group, from broad goals to particular topics, methods and resources. How adequate is an objectives model of planning of this kind of ministry of the Word?

3. Consider the preaching you have heard in your parish church over a period (say, the last couple of months). What signs does it show of planning for that ministry? What could you suggest to the preacher about ways to plan better for ministry?

4. Your teaching assignment this semester is a course of lectures on the Psalms to a small group of women interested in religious life. They have been introduced to the Bible in a general way at college. Outline your remote and proximate planning for the semester's work (not each class).

Part Two

The Ministry of Teaching the Word

Introduction

The ministry to which many students of the Word are called is the ministry of teaching. To them falls the responsibility of introducing others formally to the *koinonia* that the Bible represents, or of promoting a relationship already initiated, by programs deliberately designed for that purpose. The continuity of these programs, the contexts in which they are conducted, the preparation of the ministers, the skills, techniques, resources available to them, the intentions of the participants - all **differentiate this form of ministry** of the Word from other forms, such as preaching, so that Gregory the Great could refer to teaching as the art of arts and science of sciences.

1. Teaching as ministry

Yet to teaching as to other forms of the ministry of the Word apply equally those **principles of ministry** dealt with in Part One. Sound teaching of the Scriptures rests on a conviction of the saving purpose of the Word and a theology of revelation as *koinonia*: this Word is to be communicated, a bread to be broken, and teachers enjoy the privilege of helping in a special way this saving purpose to be achieved. In imitation of the divine considerateness, *synkatabasis*, exemplified in the Scriptures, teachers respect the readiness of their listeners for entry into the *koinonia* offered by the Word; in this they are assisted by the work of developmental scientists and learning theorists, psychologists and sociologists, as well as the recommendations of the magisterium, to preserve in their teaching the double fidelity manifested in that other, historical Incarnation - fidelity to God and fidelity to man. It is the Incarnation likewise that urges teachers to respect the cultural conditioning of both the inspired Word and its recipients, and thus to take account of factors of history, geography, race, language, sex, political and economic oppression and the like that affect modern listeners to the Word in various cultures.

At the beginning of this book we voiced the regret that advances in biblical science **in the Catholic community** this century had not everywhere been accompanied by improved communication of this growth in knowledge - hence the reason for writing. The Catholic community as a whole could not be said to be as well acquainted with the Word in his biblical form as with his other presences in the Church. For this **deprivation** and for its eventual **remedy** we must look to biblical education in the community, to the educators, and to those who should be profiting from the life-giving process.

For historical reasons, we suggested, **education of the Catholic laity** in the Bible was for centuries not given high priority in pastoral care. This emerges particularly by comparison with Protestant emphasis on the Bible and provision of programs for biblical education of adults and children. For similar reasons the **preparation of Catholic teachers** of the young, into which greater community resources were directed, did not take on a biblical character in many countries, so that teachers at this level generally are not yet comfortable with using the Bible in religious education nor do they produce RE programs for their classes that are soundly biblical. The ministry of teaching the Word to Catholics now has to take issue with this condition of neglect.

2. The teacher of the Bible

No longer in our Catholic community do teachers themselves have any excuse for inadequate preparation for ministry, except perhaps for inadequate local resources in some areas. The community since Pius XII and Vatican II has been offering formal encouragement to this ministry; no embargo lies on the best findings of scholarship for Catholic students. **The possibilities are there** for teachers of the Word to become acquainted with all the knowledge and skills necessary for the task, with that proviso of local resources. Educationists may debate the realism of a separation of content and method in this as in other areas of teaching; for clarity of exposition we have divided chapters this way, and have recommended would-be biblical educators to plan for teaching strategies, instructional media and other resources as distinct from content. We have also laboured the point that institutions preparing ministers of the Word solely through textual study without consideration of the practice of ministry are simply perpetuating the current problem. But there is no doubting the influence on teaching and learning of **the teacher's knowledge** of subject matter and his or her beliefs about the subject.

In other words, if I am to be an effective teacher of the Bible I need to know all about that book, its composition, its authors, their purpose and message, their times and background, and much more; there is an abundant literature to assist me in this quest and in my teaching role. Beyond that factual and conceptual knowledge, though, I need as well, if I am to have a thorough knowledge of the Bible, to know the explanatory frameworks that are used to guide inquiry in biblical studies and approach the text critically (the term "critically" in biblical and other literary studies being used in the sense of evaluatively, in a non-fundamentalist way). I need also to know something of the ways new knowledge of the Bible comes to the fore through research, my own or others'.

My **beliefs about the Bible** also come into play in my role as Christian educator. Of course, I believe this book is God's Word incarnate in scriptural form; hopefully, this emerges in my reverential attitude to the text, my willingness to subject it to the same literary and linguistic analysis applicable to other writings (something anathema to fundamentalists), my bias towards the theological message of these texts. My particular Catholic beliefs in the Bible will lead me to align it with, and not promote it over, those other traditional expressions of God's action (in Jesus): the liturgy, Church teaching, and other traditions of the Christian community - in other words, for me Scripture, though "sacra", is not "sola". Above all, my beliefs will emerge for my students in the enthusiasm I demonstrate in breaking the bread of the Word for

them, in opening the springs of living water. These beliefs are part
of my knowledge of the subject, and influence my teaching and
their learning - just as would an attitude of indifference or
boredom, or a tendency to regard the text as secondary to my
learned comments on it.

3. Teaching and the taught

Yet, as chapters in Part One repeatedly emphasised about
ministry in general, it is not simply the biblical text that is in focus
for the good teacher, but also **the listener to the text** and the
process of teaching. Too often, we lamented earlier, institutions
preparing ministers of the Word have neglected consideration of
these latter factors. A commendable stress has been given to
academic rigour, to the capacity of students to measure up (by
linguistic skills, for instance) to the challenge of reading ancient
biblical texts and commentaries on these in a range of modern
languages. Teaching staff have been engaged for their expertise
in individual areas of biblical science without regard for the later
teaching mission of the students.

The result has been less than adequate preparation; at best,
students of the Bible have gone forth from these institutions
equipped simply to pattern their own teaching on the style of their
mentors, irrespective of differences in levels and contexts and
ignorant of the experience and lore of educational practitioners
and researchers. This, too, is contrary to the law of incarnation,
hoping vainly that effective teaching will come to the teacher by
chance or special divine intervention without recourse to normal
and available procedures of study and practice - a particular
species of biblical fundamentalist thinking that is real, if
unconscious. It is the recipients of the message, children and
adults, college students and seminarians, who have suffered from
this unnecessary neglect. High time that equal attention was
given in biblical institutes to **the process of communication** as to
the message to be communicated. As Pius XII reminded such
places, "the sacred books were not given by God to satisfy

people's curiosity or to provide them with an object of study and research:" a share in divine life by the faithful is involved.

A case in point (to parallel Gavin Reid's imaginary college in Chapter 4). Father Rufus wonders why his Scripture lectures are not very popular with his final year seminarians. He has been entrusted with classes at this level, dealing with the book of *Revelation* in particular, on the score of his recent studies at an overseas biblical institute, and he brings to these classes a certificated expertise and a resolve to achieve a high standard of lecturing. He remembers well his own professor of exegesis at the institute, a world authority on the New Testament, who arrived punctually each morning to address his large international class, sat down, switched on the microphone, and ploughed through the Greek text verse after verse, occasionally scribbling a note on the blackboard, and left promptly as the clock struck the hour. Students had to work hard to keep up, but Father Rufus found that regular attendance and hard study paid off at the oral examination (the first time he had met the world authority personally, of whom everyone spoke in awed admiration).

Back home, however, not awe and admiration but boredom and bewilderment seem to meet Father Rufus's best efforts, though he is sure he is doing what his model did (no one at the institute having suggested any alternative). He meets his small class of Australian youth each morning, and plunges at once into a textual study of the letters to the seven churches, resisting the distraction some propose of a general discussion of apocalyptic and its similarity to current movies "The Omen" and "Apocalypse Now"; in fact, at the present rate of progress, with microscopic attention to each verse, Father Rufus isn't sure the class will get beyond those seven letters to reach the more strictly apocalyptic visions in chapters 4-21. As for movies, well, he was never much good at a blackboard, let alone anything audiovisual - but neither was the seer of Patmos, he consoles himself. It's the Word, the exegete, and the student: that's what biblical study is all about, he learnt at the institute.

By Week 6 the Word and the exegete are still hanging in there, but the students seem to have lost interest - not that he's asked their opinion: the term examination will prove his growing conviction that they are not able or willing enough for this ministry. Father Rufus is even reduced to sacrificing some time in the class to questions, but by now no one seems interested; he even finds an old chart with the seven churches of Asia fairly visible, but again interest flags. Whatever can have gone wrong? *O tempora! O mores!*

An extreme case, but perhaps not undocumented. Many a young professor, hot from the halls of learning, has subjected his or her classes to unnecessary ordeals because **no one raised issues of communication**, of purpose and perspective, of differences in needs and capacities, no one suggested a range of models of teaching and learning or highlighted differences in settings, contexts, approaches and programs. It is not by inspiration that one comes to an awareness of the variety of resources for teaching and available instructional media. Even the Ethiopian eunuch in *Acts* 8 realised that learning will not happen "unless someone shows me the way;" we shall see that the deacon Philip, if not Father Rufus's mentors, was sensitive to that in his ministry.

4. Order of treatment

So in the second part of this work on the ministry of the Word, in looking at the teaching of Scripture we shall have to address these issuess. We need to begin by facing the fact that there is a communication problem, that teachers, themselves properly resourced, need to make their knowledge of the sacred text available to others. Yet this attention to the text should not become so immediately microscopic as to obscure the general hermeneutical principles that prepare the listener for textual detail. We need to introduce students to the nature of the scriptural incarnation, and in doing so appeal not merely to reason and logic but to feeling and intuition: it is not simply transmission of information about the Bible we are seeking to achieve with people but transaction and transformation. We must also consider what is appropriate to adults and what to children **(Chapter 6)**.

Philip and the Ethiopian eunuch can guide us in the way to effect this communication: the deacon's resourcefulness, sensitivity, introduction of his listener to the whole mystery of salvation via one text are exemplary. We need to respect the models of learning appropriate to our listeners. There is also the question of the settings and contexts suited to our teaching particular groups, and approaches and programs available. Skills and techniques for work with children and adults need also be studied by the teacher of Scripture (**Chapter 7**).

The minister of the Word does not come to teaching with his or her own person as the sole resource. In addition to the text of the Word itself there are today a range of biblical resources, from critical editions and translations to commentaries and contextual studies that help teacher and student alike appreciate an ancient text. And just as today's recipients of the Word have come to benefit in their daily lives from modern communications media well beyond the printed word, so these instructional media can be employed in the teaching of Scripture, always adapting the medium to the mode of instruction; Father Rufus's formation should have alerted him to these possibilities for his ministry and trained him in their use (**Chapter 8**).

Teachers of the Word cannot be oblivious of the degree of success of their ministry: too much is at stake to allow communication to fail. The careful planning outlined in an earlier chapter must be complemented by evaluation of progress and outcomes if strengths are to be recognised and inadequacies adjusted; Father Rufus's students could have helped him during and after his course had he been willing to ask and listen, and he could have thought of assessment more comprehensively than just setting his written examination. The teacher must try to ensure that the Word of the Lord does not return empty (**Chapter 9**).

Chapter Six

Teaching the Scriptures

Outline

Scriptural *koinonia* presumes that the minister, properly resourced, can introduce the listener to the Word efficaciously. Communication of the biblical message, if it is to succeed, involves consideration of

- the place of textual study of the Bible
- the advisability of situating this within a wider perspective
- achievable goals of biblical education of adults and children, respectively.

Teaching the Scriptures, like other forms of the ministry of the Word, occurs in **various contexts**, at **various levels**, with **different approaches**. The generic term of Vatican II, "catechesis and all Christian instruction", is susceptible of division into the education of the young and the education of adults, the latter needing specification again to include basic biblical education and tertiary level education, including seminary education of those preparing for ordained ministry. Experimentation with contexts and approaches has (as we remarked in Chapter Four) characterised rather the education of the young, so that much religious education literature is directed specifically to them - which is why a problem remains particularly at the tertiary level, with the formation of those themselves preparing for ministry of some kind. Our concern in these following chapters, then, should be with biblical education at all levels, making the necessary distinctions as appropriate. (We are not concerning ourselves with biblical specialists, whose ministerial formation is presumed to be already complete - though it would not be superfluous to repeat our first principle, that the Word is by its nature to be communicated; the specialist also will at some stage need to address these questions of communication, a responsibility not always discharged.

1. A problem of communication

Communication is what this chapter is about - communication, which is one appropriate rendering of *koinonia*, translatable also as relationship, sharing. In the teaching of Scripture the Word comes to meet the person accepting him in faith; if communication does not take place, it is because the Word is impeded in its reception, or the listener is impeded. The teacher may fail to reach the student, the student may fail to appreciate the teaching; poor biblical education has resulted from each of these failings. Religious educators lament what they see as the major problem in scriptural teaching and scriptural learning; for them it is a communication problem, a curriculum problem. "Biblical research has made amazing advances in recent decades," laments one such religious educator. "Yet it becomes increasingly obvious that the wealth of knowledge currently available in the realm of biblical scholarship has somehow tragically failed to flow out into the lives and minds of adults."[1] Which suggests that the problem will be solved by **more attention to the process of communication** - *how* to teach the Bible. Another commentator asserts that "biblical scholars have an educational problem."[2]

The solution of the communication problem **is twofold**: the scholars need to be able to communicate their acquaintance with the Word, the educators need to be in touch with up-to-date biblical scholarship. Otherwise, the intended beneficiaries who come ready to drink from the living water will find nothing to slake their thirst. Happily, there are ample opportunities today for those willing to equip themselves for ministry with knowledge of the Scriptures. Here we need to concentrate on the challenge

---

[1] E. F. Trester, "Adult biblical learning in community," *Religious Education* 77 (1982) 540.
[2] M. C. Boys, "Religious education and contemporary biblical scholarship," *Religious Education* 74 (1979) 183.

that faces the resourced educator, effective communication of the biblical message.

How, then, decide what is to be communicated? Chapter Five spoke of goals and objectives which apply to the task of teaching; we need first determine *why* we are bringing this aspect of the Word to this group, and *what* we can realistically hope to achieve with them in a program we are designing. The rationale and specific instructional objectives that seem appropriate in this process of curriculum development arise, as always, out of **the needs of the group**: what aspect of the Word do these seminary students, or these Grade 5 children, need to be introduced to - close exegesis of The Chronicler's work, a parable from *Luke* 15, or some incident from Old Testament salvation history in paraphrase? Is it solid learning I should be seeking from them, or an affective response to an affecting story, or the skill of using biblical tools? In the light of these considerations I will design my program and make my decisions about the content of my sessions and the teaching strategies I will employ.

2. Textual study of the Bible

If in this chapter we approach biblical education at an adult level and not first from the viewpoint of children, it is because our intention is to influence the preparation of people for a range of teaching ministries; religious educators of children in particular have such an educational preparation. High amongst our priorities in biblical education must be introduction (at least of adults) to the text of the Scriptures for the reason that this text is the Word of God. We find no substitute for the text of *Genesis*, *Psalms*, *Isaiah*, the Gospels or Paul's letters in Chrysostom's homilies to his fourth century congregation of interested adults, who came day after day for lengthy disquisitions on a text in their own language, examined literally but (to us) uncritically.[3] Convinced and impressed though he was of the importance of his own role as scriptural commentator, Chrysostom nonetheless

---

[3] See R. Hill, "Chrysostom as Old Testament commentator," *Estudios Biblicos* 46 (1988) 61-77.

saw himself merely as an unworthy bearer of the Emperor's letters (or God's letters, at another place), of no account beside the royal text. So modern educators, too, stress the value of this **encounter with the text** by contrast with mere paraphrase.[4] (The appropriateness of the text for younger people is less obvious, as we shall see.) And today we are in a position to delve more deeply into the text than was Chrysostom himself, let alone his congregation, with the linguistic and contextual skills available to us. Hopefully the myriad commentators on our shelves have the humility to stand aside from the text like Chrysostom, and we have the sense to refer to them only as resource, not as substitute.

A modern religious educator, Mary Boys, suggests that a prime requirement of scriptural study is **attentiveness to the text**, bringing all our resources to bear on it. "To be attentive to the biblical text, for example, involves disciplining oneself to focus on *that* text, and not to be dulled by the distractions of other tasks. It means pursuing the world the text opens up, striving to hear new resonances even in familiar lines. To teach that text attentively demands turning a listening ear to the world in which we live, to the stories and concerns and questions that preoccupy students and their teachers. It also requires asking how others who live in a context different from my own might hear this text."[5]

Yet this preference for the text and its background in biblical study **should not become a fetish**. The Christian people have a right to an appreciation of the total divine plan as revealed in all the Scriptures, not simply an in-depth study of Babylonian *Ezekiel*, Old Testament primeval history, or the Infancy narratives; the riches to be imparted by the Word in his biblical *koinonia* are not exhausted by any one of these, let alone snippets of it. Some of us have suffered at the hands of erudite enthusiasts whose consuming interest in background details of, say, *Romans* or *Isaiah* has kept us so glued to the text of an opening chapter that we were never treated to the work's overall design, let alone its relevance to the author's general thought or its place in the

---

[4] Cf J. N. M. Wijngaards, *Communicating the Word of God*, 24-28.

[5] M. C. Boys, "Studying and teaching the Scriptures with imagination," *Word in Life* 38 (1990 November) 11.

total divine plan, the mystery of Christ, that the Word in its totality communicates and that we deserve to enjoy. Religious educators speak of the value of **general hermeneutical principles** that allow the student of the Bible to grasp that overall picture in addition to studying parts of the inspired text.[6] This is in keeping with the findings of learning theorists looked at earlier in Chapter Two, who tell us of the need for 'advance organisers' to our thinking, like these hermeneutical principles, if we are to accommodate a mass of new information. Father Rufus's students, we saw, begged him in vain for some general introduction to apocalyptic before plunging into the text of *Revelation* 1.1.

3. The wider view

Some impatience with the work of biblical criticism is thus understandable on the part of those who have not been allowed to see the wood for the trees, and hunger for the wider view. A balance is clearly required: biblical education - in fact, any Christian education - involves some encounter with the Word of God in the inspired text of the Scriptures, and yet inappropriate scholarly information on that text can be counter-productive. The question has been best addressed by those biblical scholars who have also looked at the educational implications of their work: how **integrate biblical scholarship with the life of faith** (we recall Augustine's similar concern). Particular strategies are suggested by them. Background information should illuminate the text, not swamp (or "flatten")[7] it: historical details of the Syro-Ephraimitic war as background to *Isaiah* should be accompanied by a general introduction to the structure of the book and the ministry of Isaiah of Jerusalem. Teachers should avoid using their knowledge of biblical criticism to bewilder people and disturb their faith; a simplistic treatment of Infancy narratives under the banner of "midrash" may not succeed in bringing people from one level of understanding to another if the teacher's motto in religious

---

[6] Cf M. C. Boys, *Biblical Interpretation in Religious Education*, 274-77; R. Hill, "The mystery of Christ: clue to Paul's thinking on wisdom," *The Heythrop Journal* 25 (1984) 475-83.

[7] A term of M. Hellwig, *Tradition: The Catholic Story Today*, Dayton: Pflaum, 1974.

education is (as one teacher admitted to me) "search and destroy". Critical study can succeed in empowering people rather than bewildering them if directed to a major change of position on a broad issue rather than to a host of minor details; developments in understanding of biblical covenant can do a lot to enlighten parents insistent on having their children's religious education rest on the Ten Commandments,[8] as we so often hear.

We might illustrate this balanced approach to the text and critical detail by a scholar sensitive to implications for religious education from the writing of a distinguished Johannine scholar, Raymond E. Brown. In an article on this task,[9] Brown sees it as vital for an understanding of the Fourth Gospel that "the audience *must* be brought into the overall Johannine thought world if they are to profit from the exposition of individual passages." Then the uniqueness of the Johannine Jesus by contrast with the other Gospels needs pointing out, especially by reference to an element totally lacking there, that "the Jesus of John is a figure who consciously and insistently speaks of a previous life before he came below, a life in which he saw and heard what he now manifests." The reader/listener to **the Gospel of John** is thus to realise that this first coming of Jesus places everyone meeting him in a state of judgement, of having to choose between light and darkness. Brown shows how to present the deeds of Jesus and the words of Jesus in John's Gospel. He insists that we do not try to dissipate the puzzlement that teacher and student alike feel with the words of Jesus: "Puzzlement is the way in which the readers/hearers are brought to recognise, however incompletely, who this Jesus is ...; when I reach lines I consider puzzling, I help the hearers to be puzzled."

A scholar as closely in touch with the text as Brown is thus in a position to provide students with those 'advance organisers' necessary for a comprehensive understanding of a biblical text; details can then be fitted into place, avoiding the correlative dangers of incomprehension and superficiality. A further danger

---

[8] R. Hill, "On first looking into *The Catechism for the Universal Church,*" *Word in Life* 38 (1990 August) 25.
[9] "The Johannine world for preachers," *Interpretation* 43 (1989) 58-65.

to be avoided in our teaching, in the view of another biblical scholar, Walter Wink, is that we apply only our reason and logic to the text and thus respond inadequately to it. "We exegetes and theologians and pastors and people haven't been using *enough* of our brains when we encounter the Bible. We have gone as far as we can in one type of specialisation - that of the left side of the brain"[10] - but have neglected our **capacity for feeling and intuition**. Teaching the Scriptures in this inadequate way may be an example of tradition or at best transaction, but fails to achieve transformation in ourselves and our listeners, because we are approaching the text only partially. Wink cites the accounts of the baptism of Jesus as examples of texts that require students to respond to images and symbols: "When we take such symbols seriously at their profound, archetypal level, they are capable of revealing depths of meaning far beyond anything we can grasp by our more usual, left-brain mode of thinking."[11] (The ambiguity in Wink's title, *Transforming Bible Study*, is thus intentional.) For Mary Boys, *Exodus* 3 on the burning bush is a similar example of a text requiring the reader's response to symbol.

Another religious educator, less concerned with historical criticism but not unaware of it, makes the following recommendations to teachers of the Scriptures:[12]
- "Approach the Scriptures, whether for study or meditation, in a spirit of prayer and anticipation."
- "Recognise any attitudes you bring to the text... Sometimes we think we have exhausted the meaning of a text because we have heard it so many times. But every text has the power and possibility for new meaning."
- "We can then become open to the text, asking the simple question, What is new?"
- "Now you need to return to the text and read it again, slowly, expectantly... Allow yourself to be *present* to the text."
- "After reading the text, it is appropriate to ask, What does this mean to me? How does it make me feel?"

---

[10] *Transforming Bible Study*, 27.
[11] *Ibid.*, 96.
[12] T. H. Morris, "Guidelines for ministers of the Word," *PACE* 18 (1987) 247-49.

- "Now is the time to become familiar with [scholarly] material (and not before the reading of the text for its personal meaning)."
- "Personal meaning and scholarly commentary must come together with the text... You and the text come together afresh."
- "We need to apply the meaning that has emerged to everyday life."
- "Only after the minister has wrestled with the text can he or she take up the responsibiity of preparing a particular application of the text for a given audience... The audience and the issues important to that audience need to be considered."
- "With all that as your foundation, you approach the text for its message and meaning for the group you are working with... You serve as a guide, a curator, and a companion."

4. Keeping the perspective wide

Yes, the ministry of teaching the scriptural Word involves introduction to the inspired text, without either making that a fetish or responding to it superficially or inadequately. But biblical education requires the teacher to open up wider questions. Since the paradigm of Incarnation must be always before us in the ministry of the Word, formal treatment of **the nature of the scriptural incarnation** is an important component of scriptural education at the appropriate level if students are to grasp questions such as biblical revelation, biblical inspiration, biblical truth, and all the cultural features of biblical texts - historical, geographical, linguistic, literary, social, sexual, religious - in some such manner as outlined in Part One above.

Obviously, too, before concentration occurs on particular biblical texts, students need introduction to **the structure of the Bible** as a whole and its principal divisions. There is rhyme and reason to the TaNaK arrangement of the Hebrew Bible; different nomenclature in "Former Prophets" and "Historical Books" is significant; the placement of *Daniel* either in The Writings or at the head of The Twelve can do with comment; the distinction between New Testament letters and General epistles needs explicating; and so on. Students who are capable of exegesis of texts need also **a knowledge of hermeneutical principles,** beginning with the ways of interpreting the Bible as a whole (the 'advance organisers' spoken of before). Are they to be satisfied with a typological approach? Should they look for some one dominating theme (e.g., covenant), or accept a man-made pattern (of Vriezen or Rowley, for instance)? Or are they capable of recognising the Pauline mystery of Christ encompassing all the Scriptures? Further, as all the enterprise of biblical *koinonia* is a theological one, accent must lie on **the theology of the Bible** and its parts; critical skills always serve the biblical message, as (on the analogy of the Incarnation) efforts to become acquainted with Jesus would fail if they did not result in recognising and confessing him to be the Christ.

Two distinguished religious educators with a solid biblical formation have approached the question of biblical education (of adults and children alike) from the wider perspective by posing **two comprehensive questions** designed to bridge the gap between scholar and student:[13]

What is this Bible which we carry?
Who are we who carry it?

Each question prompted reflections on the scriptural Word and its ministers that have implications for learning and consequently for teaching.

WHAT IS THIS BIBLE WHICH WE CARRY?	IMPLICATIONS	HOW, THEREFORE, MIGHT WE LEARN FROM IT?
Collection of ancient & diverse literature	Old, alien & distant: of particular time & culture. Work of literature	Respect the distance and specificity of the text. Read with sensitivity and imagination. Draw upon the service of specialists.
Reflection and telescoping of beliefs and experiences of communities.	Traditions functioned as living memories: past for the sake of future.	Inquire into the way the text functioned for a community.

---

[13] M. C. Boys andT. H. Groome, "Principles and pedagogy in biblical study," *Religious Education* 77 (1982) 486-507. Charts used with permission of the publisher.

Classic text	Humankind does not outgrow its issues. Has a surplus of meaning.	Wrestle with the perennial issues & concerns. Seek a totality of meanings.
Word of God in human language	Reveals a hidden God.	Expect God to be revealed.
Scripture	Sacred text for community; shapes its identity. Foundational for Jews and for Christians	Allow text to nurture, shape identity, transform. Study way text shapes different communities.

Their use of the word "carry" gives rise to comment by the authors: "The Bible is primarily a book we take with us on our life's journey, not merely a book we enshrine in a museum. It is useful for us; it nourishes us and challenges us to keep walking and talking together. As religious educators, we are not a society of antiquarians dedicated to the veneration of an old book, but a people for whom that book is vital to the way we live."[14] So, if such is the book we carry, how should we respond to it?

WHO ARE WE WHO CARRY IT?	IMPLICATIONS	HOW, THEREFORE, MIGHT WE LEARN FROM IT?
People of particular Time Class Culture Creed Sex Race	Diverse in what we bring to text and ask from it Technical rationality over "common sense" Preoccupied with historicity From many world views	Recognise and name own context. Relativize critical reason: honor common sense.
From plural and secular world	From many world views	Hear "others" from other contexts. Disciplined approach to text: Ask self-involving questions.
Members of a community of believers	Carry text to know who we are. Text primarily for community. Text interpreted over many centuries.	Place present reading in context of community over time.
Both carriers and carried, interpreters and interpreted	Text about our present and future Interpretation beyond analyzing	Text to call self/group to transformation. Text to be prayed in faith. Interpretation for decision.

---

14 *Ibid.*, 488-89.

The principles for biblical education that emerge for these educators from these basic questions are two. **Firstly**, we should bring a critical approach to the text and to ourselves and our world. We should read the text sensitively, expectantly and communally. And our approach to the text and our own situation should be made with the help of specialists, voices from the past, and voices from the "underside", those voices coming to the text from a different perspective. **Secondly**, text and experience should be brought together, each questioning the other to provide a basis for Christian praxis.[15]

The close relationship between text and reader in this approach to biblical education reflects the accent we have placed in Part One on the ministry of the Word as requiring attention both to the incarnate Word and to the readiness and cultural conditioning of the recipients of that Word if true *koinonia* is to take place.

5. Goals for adult education in the Word

Applicable though these considerations may be to serious study of the Scriptures by adults generally, both those preparing for ministry and those interested largely in self development, religious educators have also touched on some aspects of biblical education that concern students specifically in so far as they are coming to Bible study for the first time as adults; education of children presents different challenges. The key question is: what degree of biblical education can be achieved by **the general run of Catholic adults**? what blockages exist? Some years ago *Newsweek* quoted American biblical scholar Joseph A. Fitzmyer as voicing the regret about adults that "in Scripture matters, education today is so retrograde that one cannot even pose a critical question without shocking people."[16]

---

[15] *Ibid.*, 507.
[16] *Newsweek*, December 24, 1979, 49.

So there is a gap to be closed before the posing of critical questions proves to be the appropriate entry to biblical education for a vast number of people. Religious educators use terms like "anxieties" and "inner turmoil" in speaking of the effect of the Bible on many people. One writer puts their fear and uncertainty down to warnings heard from churchmen about the risk of misinterpretation; other people are simply puzzled by biblical language and customs, some shocked by behaviour found in the Bible. This writer sees Bible study as therefore a skill that will respond to '**ten commandments**' in which adults can be drilled; these may be listed here (though one might debate the acceptability of phrasing in some cases):

1. The Bible is the Word of God because it is the Church's book.

2. The Bible is "inspired by the Holy Spirit" because the Church believes that a special truth from God can be found in those writings.

3. The revealed Truth of the Bible is found in what the various writers wished to express about the meaning of faith itself.

4. Thou shalt not believe everything in the Bible (remember, the Bible is not a science book, etc.).

5. Thou shalt not take one passage from the Bible and make it an absolute (the biblical message needs to be considered in its totality).

6. Thou shalt not be surprised at finding different opinions in the Bible.

7. Thou shalt learn something about the history and literary background of the various books of the Bible.

8. Read the Bible regularly to stimulate and nourish personal faith.

9. The Bible serves as a 'religious conscience' for the Church and the individual believer.

10. The Bible does not remove the responsibility of the reader to make conscientious and responsible decisions about the faith.[17]

Partly these 'ten commandments' are rules of thumb for a reader, partly a brief for an educator involved with a group of adults;

---

[17] M. Neuman, "Ten Commandments for Catholic Bible study groups," PACE 16 (1985) "Teaching" 20-24.

their merit is that they have been found helpful with some such groups.

Another writer takes an even lower common multiple of biblical education, the response of worshippers to the Sunday readings. A sample of 300 people leaving Sunday Mass showed that none could recall the first or second readings and only twenty percent the third reading. So the suggestion is made to begin adult Bible study with the Sunday readings. We shall concentrate on ways and means in the next chapter, but it may be instructive to see **what goals are thought possible** for an adult program like this modest one:
  1) To develop the ability to read and pray with Scripture in an informed manner, relating it in a practical way to life situations.
  2) To develop abilities to share faith in Jesus and his action in lives today with other Catholic Christians.
  3) To develop a deepened understanding and appreciation of the way God has worked (in OT and NT) and is still working through his people today.
  4) To develop a desire to spread the Good News to all.
  5) To develop the regular practice of prayerful preparation of the Sunday Scripture readings.[18]
Again the approach may claim the merit of having been successful with some of the adults we see as needing help with the Scriptures if *koinonia* is to occur.

The problem does not lie on one side only. It lies with the Scriptures themselves and with informed educators (we have admitted as much), and - as some educators point out - as much with learners as with teachers. "If a major change in the landscape of adults' abilities to grasp and assimilate modern biblical scholarship in respectable depth is going to happen, it will happen only when we shift the focus from the activity of the teacher, however qualified and gifted, and begin to **refocus attention on the learners**, and what goes on when real learning

---

[18] F. Stacey, "A liturgical Bible study program," *PACE* 11 (1981) "Approaches-H" 1-4.

happens in adults."[19] Again the accent falls on process, on transaction and transformation more than on mere transmission of information in this ideal of 'adult biblical interdependent learning' (ABIL). We shall look at the process specifically in the next chapter (and in Appendix Three), but it is salutary to be reminded here of the artificiality of the distinction between content and method remarked on before; no use planning outcomes without attending also to processes. As Eugene Trester, the eminent educator quoted above, concludes, "an alternate solution to a major contemporary religious education problem for churches and synagogues lies in the development of **small communities of adult learners.**"[20]

It is only recently that the biblical education of adults other than those enrolled in tertiary institutions has been addressed seriously in the Catholic community, in many parts of the world at least. By contrast **the Protestant churches**, with their more developed theology of the Word, have placed high priority on Bible study for adults (and children) from the time of Luther and Calvin. They have lived to see this priority undermined by various factors. Two such factors have been suggested by a Protestant commentator: the destabilising effect of the spread of biblical criticism and a lowered profile of the teaching ministry. New study programs have been devised to offset this deterioration (a 'deterioration' that Catholic communities would envy, accompanied as it is by figures for regular Bible reading of between 25% and 70%!). The programs stress acquaintance with the texts and themes of the Bible, even if they disappoint that commentator (who prefers a more 'jug-to-mug' approach)[21] for stressing leadership instead of teaching, as ABIL does.

6. The Bible with children

For those historical reasons mentioned above, the Catholic community has not generally based the religious education of

---

[19] E. F. Trester, "Adult biblical learning in community," *Religious Education* 77 (1982) 542.

[20] *Ibid.*, 546.

[21] R. R. Osmer, "The study of Scripture in the congregation: old problems and new programs," *Interpretation* 42 (1988) 254-67.

children on the Bible to the extent of the reformed traditions. While it is now admitted this was an impoverishment, it at least had the incidental advantage of saving Catholic educators much of the uncertainty about **the place of the Bible in children's education** occasioned by the researches of developmentalists like Ronald Goldman claiming the support of Jean Piaget's study of children's cognitive development. Goldman investigated children's understanding of three biblical narratives - the Burning Bush, the Crossing of the Red Sea, the Temptations of Jesus - and concluded that children under the age of 13 to 14, having not attained to the Piagetian category of formal religious thinking, could not cope with that adults' book which the Bible is, and that for them a life-centred approach to religious education would be preferable to any textual study. The influence of Goldman's *Religious Thinking from Childhood to Adolesence* and *Readiness for Religion* on primary school education in the 1960s was considerable. But a decade later other researchers were holding that Goldman had inadequately claimed the support of Piaget, that primary school children, though finding parts of the Bible difficult because of inability to sequentially order events in time, could respond well to parable and allegory, myth and symbol. On the basis of work by J. Peatling and R. Murphy the view was again expressed that "a religious education programme that does not draw at all grades on the Bible is impoverished."[22]

It is ironical and seemingly perverse that the Catholic community should have been undergoing quite contrary movements of thought about the place of the Bible in religious education of children during these decades. The sixties saw the launching of **kerygmatic catechesis** promoting wholesale use of the Bible, after centuries of neglect. In the next decade, while others were reviewing Goldman's reservations, Catholic educators were by contrast finding educational grounds for questioning the efficacy of kerygma pure and undefiled, and having doubts also about **a salvation history hermeneutic** in senior RE. Not surprisingly one commentator speaks of Catholic

---

[22] A. G. McGrady, "Teaching the Bible: research from a Piagetian perspective," *British Journal of Religious Education* 5 (1983) 133.

educators' "rear-view mirror" approach to the question of the Bible in religious education in those decades.[23]

Today it may be said there is something of a consensus about **a more nuanced approach** to the use of the Bible in the religious education of children. Educators have thought more about the outcomes and experiences appropriate to them in view of developmentalists' findings and the nature of curriculum. Are we concentrating on biblical knowledge, attitudes and skills, or on the children's sense of awe and wonder at biblical narratives, or on the cultivation of biblical patterns of prayer? Some religious educators have rediscovered story in the Bible,[24] others are prepared to settle for communicating a reverence for Scripture to young children, advising against overuse of the biblical text, even of the parables. Christine Dodd offers a number of warnings about the use of the Bible with young children:

1. Don't use the Bible to threaten children: "The Bible says you mustn't..."

2. Don't take heroes from the Bible and make them out to be supermen.

3. Don't be too rigid in your use of Scripture; vary the approach.

4. Don't make the Bible too spiritual; relate it to ordinary life.

5. Don't underestimate the children's ability to take on board what Scripture is saying.[25]

Teachers of **older children** find value in the Bible for the great "diversity of religious experience, theologies, historical epochs, cultures, peoples responding to God" found there, as well as the many different images of God. Biblical study at this level should provide as well a proper contextualist understanding of people and events in terms of biblical history and culture so as to avoid that widespread simplistic fundamentalism about the Bible.[26] Some educators distinguish between learning about the

---

[23] G. Dorr, "Through a rear-view mirror? The Bible in catechetics," *The Living Light* 17 (1980) 334-40.

[24] Cf J. P. Russell, *Sharing Our Biblical Story*, Minneapolis: Winston Press, 1971, 5-16.

[25] C. Dodd, *Making Scripture Work*, 92.

[26] F. N. Weber, "Scripture for Juniors," *Today's Catholic Teacher* 21 (1988 No.7) 102; J. P. Russell, *op.cit.*, 46-71.

Bible, learning the Bible, and learning from the Bible. **Learning about the Bible** includes 1) background material, information about the daily life and customs of the people in the Bible, 2) material on the external history of the Bible, the history of its texts, translations, influence and spread throughout the world, 3) the study of the influence of the Bible upon literature or music or art. **Learning the Bible** involves introducing the pupil directly to the text of the Bible, teaching basic doctrines of the Bible, communicating a proper understanding of the biblical texts interpreted in the light of scholarship. **Learning *from* the Bible** includes both learning *about* the Bible and learning the Bible but with a different focus, being concerned mainly with the personal development of the students, and considering the Bible not as man's book about God but as God's book about man.[27]

7. Conclusion

Thankfully, there is a growing body of practical writing on teaching the Scriptures to children, by comparison with literature on other levels of biblical education. Much of this literature centres on ways and means, to which we now turn. Yet this prior question in biblical education of "what to teach" needs a lot of attention, from tertiary to the lowest elementary levels, and has **profited from much experimentation**: jumping into the text, sacred though it is, may not be what my class of seminarians, parents or infants require at this time. The other sacraments, too, are intended for particular moments in the Christian life and would be squandered elsewhere. Breaking the bread of the Word requires consideration both of the sacred text and of the listener's need.

Bibliography (for Chapters Six and Seven)
(in addition to journal articles referred to in footnotes)

M. C. Boys, *Biblical Interpretation in Religious Education*, Birmingham Al: Religious Education Press, 1980

---

[27] Editorial, *British Journal of Religious Education* 5 (1983) 111-112.

R. Charpentier, *How to Read the Old Testament/New Testament*, London: SCM, 1981

C. E. Cox, "The Bible in religious education" in N. Smart and D. Horder (edd.), *New Movements in Religious Education*, London: Temple Smith, 1975

C. Dodd, *Making Scripture Work. A Practical Guide to Using Scripture in the Local Church*, London: Chapman, 1989

M. K. Glavich, *Leading Students into Scripture*, Mystic: Twenty-Third Publications, 1987

D. L. Griggs, 20 *New Ways of Teaching the Bible*, Nashville: Abingdon, 1980

T. H. Groome, *Christian Religious Education*, Melbourne: Dove, 1980

H.-R. Weber, *Experiments with Bible Study*, Geneva: WCC, 1981

J. N. M. Wijngaards, *Communicating the Word of God*, Great Wakering: Mayhew, 1978

W. Wink, *Transforming Bible Study*, London: SCM, 1980

relevant journals: *British Journal of Religious Education*
(for Part Two)   *Catéchèse*
                 Catechesi
                 Catechist
                 Lumen Vitae
                 Religious Education
                 Religion Teacher's Journal
                 The Living Light
                 Today's Catholic Teacher
                 Word in Life

Practical exercises for ministry

1. Read again the experience of Father Rufus. How well prepared was he for his teaching role? What did he need to consider (and apparently failed to consider) before his first class with his group? To what do you put down the students' poor response to his teaching?

2. You are asked to introduce a group of high school students electing this course to the Gospel of Mark. What general hermeneutical principles will you need to apply first? Explain how you will conduct the subsequent textual study of the Gospel.

3. Have you encountered scholars/teachers who have a communication problem in regard to the Scriptures (in speaking, or even in writing)? Where does the fault lie, and how correct it? To what extent does the problem lie with you?

4. Educators these days stress the role of imagination in teaching religious matters, of bringing the right side of the brain into play, appealing to feeling and intuition. Choose a part of the Bible where failure to do this would impair biblical appreciation (by young children, for example).

Chapter Seven

"Unless someone shows me the way"

Outline

A biblical incident demonstrates the advantage of a minister skilled in leading the believer into scriptural story and text. This skilful leadership will involve attention to

- appropriate models of learning for adults and children
- the settings and contexts best suited to learning
- possible approaches and programs
- a range of ways and means already experimented with.

The *koinonia* envisaged in the utterance of the Word and its transmission in the scriptural text takes place only if the Word and the listener are not impeded in that exchange. We have seen that potential difficulties lie on either side, with the nature of the scriptural incarnation and the condition of the recipient, and that effective scriptural education depends on sound planning to break down communication barriers. A well prepared teacher can be instrumental in bringing Word and listener together in fruitful interchange; yet it is false to the Incarnation to expect this to occur without skilful facilitation.

1. A biblical exemplar

The account in *Acts* 8 of the conversion of the Ethiopian eunuch thanks to Philip's instrumentality is instructive. The eunuch, interested enough in Judaism to worship in Jerusalem and study its scriptures, was reading the text of Second Isaiah - aloud; not a simple challenge ("seated in his chariot"), rather an index of good intent. Philip, pioneer of the biblical apostolate, first endeavoured to gauge the reader's state of readiness, to which the eunuch frankly responded with an admission of ignorance and an implicit request for guidance: "How can I (understand) unless someone shows me the way?" Philip, staying with the text (thus resisting any temptation to launch into an unrelated fervorino) and invoking **sound pedagogical principles** still endorsed by biblical educators,[1] encouraged the eunuch to raise questions about the basic thrust of the passage. Only then, and "beginning with this scripture," did Philip, himself well informed on the Scriptures, move to set the passage in the wider context of the mystery of Christ. The effect was to bring the eunuch to faith and a request for baptismal confirmation. "He went on his way rejoicing," participating as he now did in that offer of life, that *koinonia*, which the Scriptures basically speak of and themselves represent.

Perhaps the incident is not typical of the ministry of the Word in being a chance encounter and not part of a sustained program resulting from the careful planning outlined above. Yet we can only wonder how different would have been the outcome, how that joyful participation in the biblical *koinonia* would not have eventuated, if Philip had not been faithful to **principles of ministry of the Word**; had he not himself already have plumbed the significance of that intriguing prophecy; had he not allowed needs to surface before plunging in unheeding; had he not taken the listener beyond the isolated text by a comprehensive hermeneusis to an appreciation of the whole mystery of salvation contained in all the Scriptures; had he not led the new believer from the living water of Scripture to the sacramental waters of baptism - from faith to faith, from sacrament to sacrament. A conspicuous exemplar of an efficacious ministry of the Word.

---

[1] W. Wink, *Transforming Bible Study*, places stress on the questions that should be directed to the text by teacher and learner.

2. Models of learning

"Unless someone shows me the way" is an appeal that validates an informed, appropriate style of teaching the Scriptures. As biblical andragogists would remind us, however, it refers directly to learning and only to teaching by implication: the style of teaching is dictated by the **preferred manner of learning** for a particular group or individual. For adults (much of the biblical data, like *Acts* 8, refers to adult settings - and again in this chapter, considering the purpose of this book, we will give prior attention to adults) that manner of learning is interdependent, collaborative, in small groups - so say the scholars who are also learning specialists.[2] That will not please those, like the commentator cited in the previous chapter criticising certain Bible study programs,[3] who believe that the secret lies in strong leadership, perhaps in the belief that "faith comes through hearing;" for them Philip was overly deliberate and might have dispensed with the opening enquiries, as do modern 'pedagogues' who come knocking on our doors. (They might reconsider the wisdom of this approach after the fatal experience of Stephen in the previous chapter of *Acts*.) Their approach does not sit well with a notion of **revelation as koinonia**, which the Scriptures themselves exemplify, nor with a process of education as transaction and transformation and not simply transmission. Our traditional lecture approach to biblical education at a tertiary level, with the teacher at centre stage, also needs reviewing in the light of these learning models.

So adults learn best by participation and enquiry and not simply by reception. An adult model of learning, though incorporating some input from the teacher as knowledgeable contributor, rests on **interchange between teacher and learner** and between learner and learner. Hence the emphasis on subjecting the

---

[2] Cf those listed by E. F. Trester, "Adult biblical learning in community," *Religious Education* 77 (1982) 545. The term 'andragogy', that Trester finds in Malcolm Knowles to balance 'pedagogy', some may cavil at as exclusive (on etymological grounds).

[3] R. R. Osmer, "The study of Scripture in the congregation: old problems and new programs," *Interpretation* 42 (1988) 254-67.

biblical text to searching questions (in the manner of Philip and the eunuch) as the basis, for example, of Wink's "transforming Bible study". For Wink, "the text, and not the leader or the group, is the focus. The Scripture is like the centre of a wheel, its spokes radiating out to individual participants. From this center both conscious and unconscious responses are aroused. Questions from the leader enable the participants to enter into **dialogue with the meaning of the text** at all levels - not just through thought, but also through feeling, intuition, even viscerally."[4] Wink helpfully suggests a series of key questions that could be put to the text of a range of pericopes illustrating Jesus on the Law, others on Parables of the Kingdom, on Jesus' Way of Healing.[5] We are reminded of Raymond Brown's manner of introducing readers to John's Jesus in the Fourth Gospel: "Puzzlement is the way in which the readers/listeners are brought to recognise, however incompletely, who this Jesus is...; when I reach lines I consider puzzling, I help the readers to be puzzled."[6]

Philip's joining the eunuch in a study of the Isaian text on the Suffering Servant shows that the Old Testament is equally susceptible of a questioning approach applied to it by a small group of learners. "When we rediscover the questions that have themselves evoked the text, and follow them back to their source; when we enter into the shared struggle to comprehend what is moving in the question, and bring to it not only the left brain - the thinking, choosing, rational part of the self - but also the right brain, **including the intuitive and emotional and imaginative aspects** of the psyche; when we are willing to suspend our favorite beliefs (and disbeliefs), our most cherished convictions and our most authoritative doctrines, in order to listen for what might be speaking to us from the texts - then it sometimes happens that a spark leaps the gap."[7] This phrase reminds us that Chrysostom

---

4 *Transforming Bible Study*, 37.

5 *Ibid.*, ch.9.

6 "The Johannine world for preachers," *Interpretation* 43 (1989) 63.

7 W. Wink, *Transforming Bible Study*, 42.

(who did not require his congregation to suspend their beliefs or the community's "authoritative doctrines") was nonetheless insistent on **the text's ability to enlighten the listeners**: "Here am I, lighting the fire of Scripture and the lamp of its teaching is enkindled on my lips"[8] - though the lack of interchange in the homiletic context and approach in fact explains the inattention that provoked his rebuke; like teaching, the ministry of preaching the Word has particular challenges in achieving true *koinonia*.

3. Settings, contexts, approaches, programs

This is why much modern comment on effective ministry of the Word focuses on context and setting as an important factor in learning. It may be appropriate for institutions, like schools and colleges, to conduct biblical study in classrooms and lecture halls accommodating large groups; even there, however, if the process of teaching and learning is to go beyond mere transmission and reach a transaction and transformation that respects the scriptural *koinonia*, **some interchange is involved**. At least for adults, a community setting and the possibility of sharing are required; for that even the parish worshipping community can be unsuited, as Chrysostom found in the early Church. The reasons for this are not only human and theological, as outlined above. William Riley, taking Mark's Gospel as example and tracing its composition in the second century account of Papias of Hierapolis, finds that this Gospel is primarily community material: it was received by a community of faith, it was drawn up with their needs in mind, it was transmitted through the community. Papias's words about Peter's preaching and Mark's recording it (as reported by Eusebius)[9] say as much. For Riley it follows that study of the Gospel should be in a community context: "The ways in which we saw the community at work in the formulation of Mark's Gospel can give us some guidelines, some pointers toward what should be

---

[8] Sermon 4 on *Genesis* (*PG* 54,597).
[9] *Historia Ecclesiastica* 3,39,15 (*SC* 31, 156-57).

happening in the group study of Scripture in general, and Mark in particular."[10] Christians should receive and study the Gospel in community; they should see their own situation and needs as analogous to those of Mark's community; they should validate its message for themselves as a community; **as a community they should interact** with the Gospel material, share this with one another and pass it on to others.

Experience also has shown that these outcomes are realisable particularly in small group situations - **Bible study groups** variously organised. They have a good track record in recent times, and the literature reporting their success is abundant, though as early as the fourth century Chrysostom was exhorting his congregation to ruminate on his formal textual commentary in more intimate settings:

> On your part, keep in mind what we've been saying, remember it, teach it to those who did not hear it, and let each of you ponder it, whether in church, in the street or at home... We will be able while at home, before dining or after dining, by taking the sacred books in hand, to gain benefit from them and provide spiritual nourishment for our soul.[11]

The same factors of small numbers and informal setting operate today to make the small home study group an effective context for Bible study.[12] Requiring no highly qualified personnel or elaborate administration, Bible study groups can be organised in any locality, providing interested people with an unthreatening introduction to the Word that is likely to lead to a desire for deeper study. A missioner in the Philippines reports the huge success of such "Bible Sharings" that started from general ignorance, one enthusiast and

---

[10] "The Gospel of Mark: why the community should reclaim its property," *Scripture in Church* 14 (1984) 469. Cf his *The Bible Group: An Owner's Manual*, Dublin: Veritas, 1983.

[11] Sermon 8 on *Genesis* (*PG* 54,619); homily 10 on *Genesis* (*PG* 53,90).

[12] Cf W. Husson, "A practical model for adult Bible learning," *Religious Education* 77(1982) 534-39.

a Bible: "Eventually we had 2000 people having the Bible Sharing [in groups] every week. They came together in the school, in their own streets or neighbourhood, at a time agreeable to all, and did their Bible Sharing for one and a half hours weekly; they sometimes forgot the time and went on for more than two hours."[13] On the other hand, practised participants warn that basic organisation is required, and therefore time and energy, as well as some guidance (and perhaps suitable materials) if groups are to avoid falling into pitfalls like fundamentalism and obnoxious group dynamics.

What is being aimed at in small group study of the Bible may vary according to the wishes and background of the participants. One experienced leader examines **three possible approaches**: the formal, scholarly study of Scripture is thought inappropriate, the pious, devotional study inadequate and possibly harmful; so preference goes to "the Scripture as a source of understanding and life, of 'practical truth and love': historical, literary and theological dimensions of Scripture are studied because they help to shed light on the deeper message of the Old and New Testaments. The emphasis is on probing the deepest meaning of the text in the light of the author's intent and the community process of formation through which the writings took shape."[14]

Perhaps choice of one approach, one outcome or another will determine also **the kind of program** followed in a Bible study group. Partly for the reason that experience has shown that Sunday congregations emerge from Mass uncomprehending or unmindful of what was read a few minutes before, some parish ministers have adopted a program based on the Sunday readings

---

[13] A. Kelly, "Opening up through the Bible. Transformation through the Bible in parish and school," *Scripture in Church* 14 (1984) 102-103.

[14] D. Bader, "Studying the Bible: a five-year program," *PACE* 12 (1982) "Approaches-A" 1-2.

over the three-year cycle;[15] one goes so far as to recommend, on the basis of experience, "adopting the Church year and the Lectionary as curriculum in the local church" for all parish activities.[16] William Riley, quoted above, has found on the contrary that "the liturgical reading of Mark is fragmented and episodal," and he recommends a more sequential program for the Bible study group.[17] Others have therefore adopted long-term programs aimed at systematic study of the whole Bible.[18]

Any such program for Bible study in small groups calls for some degree of **planning and organisataion**, especially if pitfalls are to be avoided. Experienced ministers of the Word such as those quoted above arrange for training or briefing of facilitators to ensure the groups run smoothly and succeed in meeting the Word - something the eunuch found does not happen "unless someone shows the way." Text materials have been developed as a result of these groups' experience, and a range of them is available at various levels of sophistication (as perusal of works cited here will indicate). There is, however, no substitute for the inspired text of the Word: it is remarkable how people generally (I used think only Catholics are guilty of this until I began teaching also in a secular university) can come to listen to Bible study *sans* Bible, ready to read a text about the Bible or listen to someone speak about it. **Crossing the physical barrier** is primary (at least for adults) - getting people to purchase a suitable Bible, bring it to sessions, open it and (without reference to Table of Contents or - worse still - marginal tabs) find their way around Old and New Testaments. Until that happens habitually, the Bible remains literally a closed book. (See Appendix Three on Bible groups.)

---

[15] Cf F. Stacey, "A liturgical Bible study program," *PACE* 11 (1981) "Approaches-H" 1-4.

[16] V. Eckley, "The Church year and the Lectionary as curriculum for the local church," *Religious Education* 77 (1982) 554-67.

[17] Art.cit., 468.

[18] Cf D. Bader, "Studying the Bible: a five-year program".

4. Ways and means

Which suggests there is still a role for the teacher in Bible study, whether andragogue or pedagogue, whatever of the proven success of the small group for (adult) sharing, *koinonia*. There are a myriad **skills and techniques** that have been developed by resourceful educationists for bringing beginners to an acquaintance with the biblical text, aside even from the greatest resource of all (after the inspired text itself), the person of a well-prepared, enthusiastic guide in the tradition of deacon Philip. The skills begin with familiarisation with the sacred text (as long as familiarity does not breed contempt; Chrysostom and his fellow Eastern pastors have left us a salutary lesson in reverence for the Word incarnate in the inspired pages), and familiarisation with biblical tools - concordances, dictionaries, atlases, synopses, harmonies, even lexicons[19] (we shall deal more fully with resources for biblical education later). Educationists speak of the skills of interpretation, narration, description and decoding of the text: knowing how to determine the meaning of a text, mastering the art of story telling, expressing ourselves in visual language, reading Scripture to others in such a way that the message is fully understood.[20] At another level, of course, there are linguistic skills, exegetical and hermeneutical sills, and a range of critical skills higher and lower that are acquired with great effort and that are appropriately applied by the minister of the Word in some situations.

The Bible offers the student such a range of forms of expression, some foreign to us, that a creative teacher has plenty of scope for developing **appropriate learning techniques**. Children and adults have been led in playing the role of biblical characters - Zacchaeus, Nicodemus, Martha and Mary, the disciples on the

---

[19] Cf. D. L. Griggs, *20 New Ways of Teaching the Bible*, 7-11.
[20] Cf J. N. M. Wijngaards, *Communicating the Word of God*, 11.

way to Emmaus, Peter at the Transfiguration.[21] For these
teachers, role playing and other forms of dramatisation have
involved participants to an extent greater than mere talk could
make possible; there is still need, though, it might be added, to
remain clear as to our objectives in such stratagems. Other
teachers have found success in getting students to write a psalm on
the model of the canonical psalms,[22] or write their own Gospel[23]
(with directions as to the kind of material that should be included -
Passion narrative, some parables, some miracle stories, etc.). A
former missioner to India, John Wijngaards, has developed a
range of techniques for use not just in foreign climes but by
teachers and catechists everywhere;[24] teaching the Scriptures is a
missionary endeavour in all our churches with all Christians, not
only with Ethiopian eunuchs and Indian seminarians. These
techniques could be listed here as having survived the test of
experience; they seem applicable to all ages, but some have been
found more helpful with different groups.

(a) with younger children

1. simple free narration (e.g., Rehoboam's rejection of advice: *1 Kings* 12.1-
   9)
2. simple portrait (e.g., Absalom: *1 Samuel*)
3. commentated reading (e.g., *Isaiah* 51.1-3)
4. reading illustrated by acting (e.g., Ezekiel's vision of dry bones: *Ezekiel*
   37.1-14)
5. one point example (e.g., Joshua's deception by the Gibeonites: *Joshua* 9.1-
   18)

(b) with older children

6. story-reflection-story (e.g., the Fall: *Genesis* 2.5 - 3.24)

---

[21] Cf M. M. Hill, "Role-playing: bringing Scripture characters to life," *PACE* 16 (1986) 171-
73.
[22] F. N. Weber, "Scripture for Juniors," *Today's Catholic Teacher* 21 (1988 April) 102.
[23] D. L. Griggs, *op.cit.*, 51-52; J. Navone, "Write a Gospel," *Review for Religious* 38 (1979)
668-73.
[24] *Op.cit.*, 14-16 and *passim*.

7. portrait-reflection (e.g., the Queen of Sheba: *1 Kings* 10)
8. exposition of a motif (e.g., hospitality: *Luke* 7.44-47; 10.38-42; 19.1-10)
9. imaginative elaboration (e.g., Amos's preaching: *Amos* 4.1-3)
10. giving witness (e.g., to a sense of forgiveness: *Luke* 7.36-50)

(c) with mixed ages

11. a mystery ramble (e.g., the story of Zacchaeus: *Luke* 19.1-10)
12. spotlight exegesis (e.g., the lilies of the field: *Luke* 12.27)
13. reflection on a proverb (e.g., *Proverbs* 27.5)
14. reflection on a law (e.g., *Deuteronomy* 24.5)
15. comparative Gospel study (e.g., Beatitudes in *Matthew* 5 and *Luke* 6)
16. theological perspective (e.g., Melchizedek's offering: *Genesis* 14.18-20)

5. The Bible with children

As mentioned above, religious educators of young and older children have experimented more widely and adopted more responsively the findings of teaching and learning theorists. They have generally thought out appropriate learning models and made adjustments to settings and contexts for learning. Catholic teachers are becoming more comfortable with the Bible and producing more biblically based programs. So it is not surprising that the literature suggesting ways and means of biblical education of children is more abundant and full of practical detail. These **tips by specialist religious educators** such as Christine Dodd and Mary Kathleen Glavich go beyond the more general, more heady suggestions of an Indian missioner; Glavich's ideas for teaching the Bible are numerous, down to earth, and obviously the fruit of experience with children:

1. Read the Bible; put it in children's hands.
2. Proclaim the good news - clearly, powerfully, reverently.
3. Tell the stories in the Bible.
4. Dramatize the situations in Scripture.

5. Relate God's Word to the world.
6. Correlate Scripture with the arts.
7. Share personal impact of Scripture.
8. Rewrite Scripture prayers.
9. Research biblical topics.
10. Create scriptural art; decorate with verses from Scripture.
11. Add humour to Scripture study.
12. Sing Scripture-based songs.
13. Dance in response to Scripture.
14. Memorise to master the material; memory aids.
15. Discuss Scripture for insights; types of discussions.
16. Write on the Word of God.
17. Pray using the Scriptures.
18. Simulate biblical events.
19. Collect Bible-related materials.
20. Play Bible games.
21. Use audiovisuals to spark Bible studies.
22. Computerise Bible lessons.
23. Celebrate sacred Scripture.
24. Apply God's Word to life.[25]

The Scriptures themselves in their rich variety are an encouragement to biblical educators to adopt a variety of ways and means of breaking the bread of the Word to ready recipients. Chrysostom pondered often the divine considerateness, *synkatabasis*, exemplified in the Scriptures, and he suggested how ministers of the Word might likewise adopt an inventive considerateness:

As I've repeatedly said (and will never cease repeating constantly), God adjusts the language to suit the limitations of his listeners. His anxiety, you see, is not to ensure at the time that

---

[25] *Leading Students into Scripture, passim.*

what he says is in keeping with respect due to God but that it can be grasped by them. So he gradually leads them upwards; yet instead of remaining at the level of earthly realities, he opens up other more elevated senses.[26]

Yes, the Word incarnate in the Scriptures is **a stimulating paradigm** for a creative ministry of the Word. This creativity should come to characterise adult biblical education to the extent that religious educators of children have succeeded in being creative ministers.

Bibliography (see Chapter Six)

Practical exercises for ministry

1. Read *Acts* 8.26-40 as a model for the ministry of the Word. What can we learn from it of ways to approach our teaching mission? Rewrite the incident in terms of a situation and times closer to our own.

2. Have you had a good experience of ABIL - adult biblical interdependent learning? Compare that experience with other teaching experiences of yours for effectiveness. Do you agree interdependent, collaborative learning in small groups suits adults best for biblical education? for all needs?

3. You are briefing group leaders for adult Bible study. Point out what they need to keep in mind in conducting their weekly Bible group in view of the objectives you have set. How much room is there for being creative?

4. If you are a teacher of children, what ways and means of teaching the Bible have you found effective? Are there other procedures you could adopt?

---

[26] Homily on *Psalm* CXX (*PG* 55,303).

Chapter Eight

Resources and media for teaching

Outline

Biblical education today can take advantage of aids to teaching developed since the invention of printing up to modern computer technology. These include

- resources which illuminate the printed text, and
- those that shed light on its context; plus
- a range of instructional media.

Effective use of these presupposes the ability to match them to the mode of instruction, competence in their operation, and evaluation of their success.

Successful exercise of the ministry of teaching the Scriptures depends on decisions regarding communication of the biblical message, including attention to the text of the Scriptures and adoption of a wider perspective in which to situate the text. These are basic decisions on what can and should be taught to particular groups and individuals. Judgement is also required on the appropriate model of learning to be followed, on appropriate settings and contexts, approaches and programs, whether for adults or children, on ways and means of teaching that have been found effective in particular situations by experienced ministers of the Word.

We found examples even in apostolic and patristic practice of such judgement on the teaching of Scripture and the ways to achieve it. What was not available to Philip and the Fathers, however, is the great range of **aids to teaching and learning** that have been developed for scriptural education in recent times. The invention of printing in particular made possible the dissemination of a myriad resources devised by biblical scholars for plumbing the biblical text and its message. Modern technology has improved their utility, and has developed in addition various means or media or communication that enrich the process of education, including biblical education.

1. Resources for biblical education

The principal resource for the ministry of the Word is, of course, **the Word itself in its scriptural form** - even if we have to add the caveat that reading the text is more appropriate at some ages than others. Countless Christians and Jews have been nourished in their spiritual growth by the uncomplicated reading of the Bible. The ideal of piety among Protestant congregations in particular has been summed up as "every man sitting down with his Bible in front of him."[1] Calvin phrased it this way: "Let this be a firm principle: No other word is to be held as the Word of God, and given place as such in the church, than what is contained first in the Law and the Prophets, then in the writings of the apostles; and the only authorized way of teaching in the church is by the prescription and standard of his Word."[2]

We found the Ethiopian eunuch, however, in that favoured position, Bible open in front of him, yet complaining, "How can I understand unless someone shows me the way?" So it should also be added as axiomatic that good biblical education will often require also the resource that is **an informed and skilful minister of the Word**; the urgency of this further need constitutes the basis of that ministry. Philip and the Fathers provided us with examples of

---

[1] E. Käsemann, "Thoughts on the present controversy about scriptural interpretation," *New Testament Questions of Today*, London: SCM, 1969, 268.

[2] *Institutes of the Christian Religion*, Vol.21, Philadelphia: Westminster, 1960, 1155.

such resourceful ministers, both informed themselves and skilful enough to facilitate and not obstruct the relationship that is true biblical *koinonia*.

1) the text

With that proviso, then, that a guide for the way may be necessary and irreplaceable, we begin with the scriptural text as basic resource for biblical education. What the passage of time and cultural development have ensured is the ready availability of the text of the Bible, in the original languages and in translation in as many as 1928 modern languages (in a count made by the Bible Societies in 1989). Only for the scholar will **the original text** prove a real resource, yet it is on these critical editions (critical in the sense of being based on evaluation of the best manuscripts) that our confidence in reading the Word in translation rests. The work of archeologists and textual critics has thus made available to us the most complete form of the text recognisable to this point in history; for the Old Testament the *Biblia Hebraica Stuttgartensia*,[3] and for the New Testament the *Novum Testamentum Graece* edited by E. Nestle and K. Aland.[4] What we need and what is available to us less expert students of the Word in the task of evaluating and comparing the relative merits of resources such as editions of the original texts is a **bibliography** of biblical materials; two have been published by the Biblical Institute Press in Rome, *Basic Tools of Biblical Exegesis* by S. B. Marrow (2nd ed., 1978) and *An Introductory Bibliography for the Study of Scripture* by J. A. Fitzmyer (3rd ed., 1990).

If the text of the scriptural Word is our basic resource in teaching, it is accessible to most students in translation; and thanks to the diligence of scholars and the Bible societies, a range of **translations** exists in all modern languages. Choice of a suitable translation for study is important, and it depends on the same

---

[3] Ed. K. Elliger and W. Rudolph, Stuttgart: Deutsche Bibelstiftung, 1967-77.
[4] Stuttgart: Deutsche Bibelstiftung, 1979, 26th ed.

criteria adopted by the translators. We have examined above in Chapter Three some of the factors considered by translators endeavouring to render the text of the Word incarnate in the culture of one people at one time into the situation of people of different cultures today.[5] There is also the difference between literal and free translations, or what translators call the principles of 'formal correspondence' and 'dynamic equivalence':[6] the one is employed when it is thought appropriate to keep close to the exact expression and even to the rhythms of the original author, while the latter takes liberties in favour of patterns in the modern language. The translators have in mind the different levels of readers and listeners (whether serious students or beginners, adults and children) and the different purposes to which the text is being put (liturgical reading, biblical study, catechesis at various levels). Our choice (of an English translation, e.g.), whether for the more literal *Revised Standard Version* or for the freer *Good News Bible*, depends on similar criteria; even so, 'dynamic equivalence' runs the risk of unacceptable distortion of the author's meaning (cf Fitzmyer's evaluation of *TEV*).[7] A paraphrase of the text, of course, (like *The Living Bible*) is different again. There may also be times when we wish to refer to the **ancient versions** of the Old Testament like the Greek Septuagint, or the Latin versions of the New Testament, the Old Latin or Jerome's Vulgate, not to mention ancient versions in other languages.

Whether we are using the original text or a translation, there are other resources available for plumbing the author's meaning. Exegesis of a passage in translation or original text can call upon **lexica** of those languages or of ancient versions to throw light on word meanings. **Concordances** provide the service of listing all occurrences of particular words so as to fill out their complete denotation and connotation, with the proviso that a concordance

---

[5] Cf E. A. Nida, W. D. Reyburn, *Meaning Across Cultures*, Maryknoll: Orbis, 1981.

[6] Cf W. A. Hutchinson, "Selecting a Bible: which translation?" *The Living Light* 17 (1980) 350-56.

[7] *An Introductory Bibliography for the Study of Scripture*, 43.

of a particular translation depends for its reliability upon the consistency of the translator if we are to get a faithful picture. In study of the Gospels in particular, a **synopsis** can be handy in laying out parallel passages to help us see the evangelists reporting incidents differently; they are available in the original and in translation. **Dictionaries** of the Bible differ from lexica in including entries on all matters referred to in the Bible, not simply linguistic matters. Reference to a bibliography, as mentioned before, will enable the student to choose the particular resource that best suits needs or provides the most up-to-date service.

The biblical text, thus resourced, lies before the student awaiting study. The Bible, however, is not simply a book but a library of books; finding one's way around that library does indeed require "someone to show me the way." Again resources are available in the form of **Introductions** - to the Bible as a whole and to each testament. An Introduction, despite the name, is not necessarily an elementary book; in fact, it can be extremely scholarly, including all the latest information on particular books - authorship, condition of the text, ancient versions, literary structure, time and place of composition, history of interpretation, etc. - plus a bibliography of studies of the book. So an Introduction to the Old Testament, for example, is a mine of information on each OT book and the way it has been studied; not to consult such a resource before beginning our own study of the book would be knocking on doors already open or at least ajar. Again, there is a range of such resources, more or less scholarly and detailed.

Taking up from where the Introduction leaves off in the task of bringing us into touch with the scriptural text is the **commentary** on a particular book. While a commentary may begin by summarising information about origin and contents in the manner of an Introduction (and some commentaries thus become truly Introductions as well, like *The New Jerome Biblical Commentary*),[8] its principal work is to comment on the text of the

---

[8] Ed. R. E. Brown et al, Englewood Cliffs: Prentice Hall, 1990.

book, whether in the original language or in translation, proceeding verse by verse, bringing out the thought of the author. The commentary provided may not always be as thorough as to constitute complete exegesis or explanation of the author's thought against the background of his time; Chrysostom, for instance, in commenting on the Fall in *Genesis* was content to bring out particularly the text's moral significance. Exegesis, by contrast, would focus upon textual and linguistic matters, literary and historical issues arising from the text, and thus be in a position to arrive at a statement of the author's vision and theological message. As not all these specialised skills belong to all of us, we are much indebted to sound commentaries on books of the Bible, choosing the level of commentary that suits our needs and our own competencies.

2) the text in context

With these resources to hand, we are about ready to begin an informed study of the text and introduce others to it in our teaching; the Ethiopian eunuch would have been glad to have such tools available for his study of Deutero-Isaiah. We have before us not only the text but now also a considerable background to it that sheds light on it; we do not need St Thomas to tell us that the part makes most sense when studied in the context of the whole. It may be that our text is still obscure, and our commentary does not go far enough in supplying historical or geographical information to resolve the problem. Predictably, there exist also specialist studies in these areas, particularly **histories** of biblical times and descriptions of biblical practices and institutions. A biblical **atlas** will provide maps of biblical lands in ancient times and of the corresponding archeological sites today. A further resource that backgrounds the text for us is the collection of **other literatures** of the biblical period providing an illuminating comparison between canonical and non-canonical composition, such as that of the ancient civilisations of Egypt and Mesopotamia, the pseudepigraphical works of the intertestamental period, literature from Qumran, rabbinic commentaries, and the range of gnostic writings. We would certainly then be in a position to make a contextual study of the Bible.

All this information available to us in our study of the biblical text must not distract us from our primary purpose: to meet the Word incarnate in the text, to achieve biblical *koinonia*. Our study and our teaching is thus primarily theological, to detect the revelation of himself that God is giving us in the text; to ignore this in the process of assembling other information about the text would be a travesty of the *koinonia* that Scripture represents. How do we detect this message of our particular text, the message of Old Testament and New Testament, the message of the Bible as a whole? Again resourcing is available in the body of **hermeneutical literature** that studies the way the text has been and should be interpreted, and in works of **biblical theology** that highlight the theological message of the text. Interpretation, including theological interpretation, is a rather more subjective process than compiling dictionaries and concordances, and there are thus various schools of biblical theology; a scriptural bibliography will alert us to the directions and quality of such publications. Our own response to the text, of course, is basic, but the work of other scholars will supplement our response. That is what resources are for, and Bible study has been generously supplemented in this way.

2. Instructional media

As mentioned above, the invention of printing promoted the study of Scripture by making available texts and translations, taken advantage of more actively by some Christian traditions than others, as well as an abundance of other printed resources. The preached word and the printed text, however, have long since ceased to be the only means of teaching and learning available for the study of Scripture; "I saw it in black and white" is no longer the last word on the process. Modern technology has provided a wide range of instructional media for education. Today's youngsters and young adults have grown up in **a multimedia environment** to an extent not always accepted by older educators; Father Rufus would have done well to acknowledge this in his teaching. "By the time a youth graduates from high school today, he has viewed approximately fifteen-thousand hours of television, has attended five hundred feature motion pictures, and has had, in addition, a constant background of radio and records. During the same years, he has spent just eleven-thousand hours in school."[9] The modern home, at least in the developed countries, is a veritable information centre, boasting more than one (colour) television set (complete with VTR: videotape recorder), with as many as eight or nine radios in the house and car or strapped to the person of the occupants, not to mention the newspapers and magazines that come into the home. Parents along with their children are affected.

Education centres, then, from elementary schools to universities, have had to compete with the home information centre for the attention of the learner in this multimedia age; and they have naturally taken advantage of these media for instruction (it is thus no longer a question of a few optional "aids"). They are so numerous as to be divisible into **families of instructional media** (or presentation media): non-projected graphic and print media (including books, handouts, charts, posters, chalk boards/white boards), projected visuals (including filmstrips, slides, overhead projector transparencies), simple audio and audiovisual media (including radio, records, tape recorders, slide-tape presentations), films, television, computers, databases.

One way these may be set out is as follows:[10]

---

[9] J. B. Haney, E. J. Ulmer, *Educational Communications and Technology*, 2.
[10] *Ibid.*, 17. Used with permission.

PRESENTATION FORM	MEDIA FAMILY	PRESENTATION MEANS
Still-visual	1. STILL PICTURES, AND GRAPHICS	Direct Display
	2. STILL PROJECTION	Optical Projection
Audio	3. AUDIO tape recordings disc recordings	Electronic Playback
	radio telephone	Telecommunications
Audio plus still visual	4. SOUND-VISUAL sound filmstrip sound slide series	Electronic playback + optical projection
	sound page (book) audio card	Electronic playback + direct display
Motion-visual	5. MOTION PICTURE silent motion picture	Optical projection
Audio plus motion-visual	sound motion picture	Electronic playback + optical projection
Audio plus still visual	6. TELEVISION still picture television	Telecommunications
Audio plus "moving line" visual	telewriting	and Electronic playback (when using recorded source)
Audio plus motion visual	video television	

The table does not take account of the immense instructional resources now available on computer **databases**, such as CD-ROM (Compact Disc - Read Only Memory) capable of packing into a fraction of one disc a 20-volume Bible dictionary and an equal amount of cross-referencing - a great resource for learning in biblical as in other areas; what was previously available in print, such as concordances and indexes, is now more readily accessible on computer. **Computers** have proved their value for learners, teachers, textbook authors, researchers. Beyond their obvious utility for information storage and retrieval, they can function as assessment tool when programmed to provide certain testing procedures, as a management aid in keeping records and computing grades, as a development system in organising knowledge, as a study aid, as a tool for research.[11] Computers are a resource and a medium of instruction to be taken advantage of by biblical scholars and teachers. They can be combined with other media, such as slide projectors and videos, to produce multi-screen audiovisuals and split-screen effects; the overhead projector can be linked to computer for helpful classroom graphics.[12] Father Rufus's alma mater would have done him (and his students) a service to alert him to these possibilities.

3. The role of instructional media

If we are teaching the Bible to today's audiences, congregations, classes, groups or individuals, we must be aware of the opportunity and the challenge that all these media represent: **an opportunity** to enrich our teaching, **a challenge** to reach the learners in ways no less effective than they are affected in other areas of teaching and learning. No longer is the printed text (even if supplemented by chalk and talk!) keeping pace with educational technology; it is significant that, in the table above, the book does not even rate a mention by the compilers, an understandable if unfortunate omission. Just as in Chapter Four we acknowledged that the ministers of the Word today must utilise a range of settings, contexts and approaches, and not be content with those that are inadequate if traditional, like lecture halls and large churches, so exclusive reliance on one instructional medium, like the printed word, is not being faithful to the requirements of **an incarnational ministry in today's world.**

In the nature of things, it is likely that the minister of the Word who is ready to adapt the learning situation to the needs of

---

[11] N. Smart, "Computers in Education," *The Encyclopaedia of Educational Media Communications and Technology*, 149-53.

[12] A. J. Romiszowski, *Developing Auto-instructional Materials*, 379-80.

the particular group will also endeavour to **match instructional media to modes of instruction**. The mass lecture, the more intimate shared learning session, discussion period, tutoring, elementary class teaching, independent study call for or allow for employment of different instructional media. Photographic material, maps, charts, tables suit a small group but may be invisible at the back of a large lecture hall; likewise a single TV monitor. The overhead projector has proved its adaptability to a range of situations and needs. Larger institutions can offer the resources of an educational technology team to provide the multi-media and split-screen effects that the parish minister of the Word in the local hall may not be able to reach to with his or her small group. And so on. The relative **advantages and limitations of instructional media** have been set out as follows:[13]

Material	Advantages	Limitations
Photographic print series	1. Permit close-up detailed study at individual's own pacing. 2. Are useful as simple self-study materials and for display. 3. Require no equipment for use.	1. Not adaptable for large groups. 2. Require photographic skills, equipment, and darkroom for preparation.
Slide series	1. Require only filming, with processing and mounting by film laboratory. 2. Result in colourful, realistic reproductions of original subjects. 3. Prepared with any 35mm cameras for most uses. 4. Easily revised and updated. 5. Easily handled, stored, and rearranged for various uses. 6. Increased usefulness with tray storage and automatic projection. 7. Can be combined with taped narration for greater effectiveness. 8. May be adapted to group or to individual use.	1. Are relatively difficult to prepare locally 2. Require special equipment for close-up photography and copying. 3. Can get out of sequence and be projected incorrectly if slides are handled individually.

---

[13] A. J. Romiszowski, *The Selection and Use of Instructional Media*, 98. Used with permission.

Filmstrips	1. Are compact, easily handled, and always in proper sequence. 2. Can be supplemented with captions or recordings. 3. Are inexpensive when quantity reproduction is required. 4. Are useful for group or individual study at projection rate controlled by instructor or user. 5. Are projected with simple lightweight equipment.	1. Are relatively difficult to prepare locally. 2. Require film laboratory service to convert slides to filmstrip form. 3. Are in permanent sequence and cannot be rearranged or revised.
Recordings	1. Easy to prepare with regular tape recorders. 2. Can provide applications in most subject areas. 3. Equipment for use, compact, portable, easy to operate. 4. Flexible and adaptable as either individual elements of instruction or in correlation with programmed materials. 5. Duplication easy and economical.	1. Have a tendency for over-use, as lecture or oral textbook reading. 2. Fixed rate of information flow.
Overhead transparencies	1. Can present information in systematic, developmental sequences. 2. Use simple-to-operate projector with presentation rate controlled by instructor. 3. Require only limited planning. 4. Can be prepared by variety of simple, inexpensive methods. 5. Particularly useful with large groups.	1. Require special equipment, facilities and skills for preparation. 2. Are large and present storage problems.
Videotape/ videocassette	1. Permit selecting the best audiovisual media to serve program needs. 2. Permit normally unavailable resources to be presented. 3. Playback capability of video recording permits analysis of on-the-spot action.	1. Do not exist alone, but are part of total television production. 2. Must fit technical requirements of television.
Multi-media presentations (e.g., slide /tape)	1. Combine presentation of slides with other media forms for presentations. 2. Use photographs, slides, filmstrips and recordings in combination for independent study. 3. Provide for more effective communications in certain situations than with only a single medium.	1. Require additional equipment and careful coordination during planning, preparation, and use.

Doubtless, subject matter also affects our choice of appropriate, helpful presentation media. Biblical **archeologists** and **geographers** long ago discovered the camera, and their presentations have benefited from the photographs and slides made by themselves and other researchers. Biblical **historians** have employed their charts for timelines and maps. Does that mean that exegesis, biblical theology and language study are confined to the spoken word and use of a printed text? We have all had the experience of lectures delivered without interruption to the flow of words and unrelieved by employment of any other instructional media than printed note material. There is no need for that today; beyond the (limited) visual impact of chalk and white boards, which can be effective with skilled practitioners, there is available at least the overhead projector (OHP), which can provide variety in supplanting the printed outline and allows for gradual development of a presentation with the use of felt pens or a series of prepared overlays. In addition, even the barest **exegetical** or **theological** presentation can be enriched by the use of filmstrips, slide sequences, audio tapes and videos that have been professionally prepared, are readily available and help the contextual task of exegesis spoken of in our previous listing of printed resources; Solomon's Temple or The Chronicler's Jerusalem, Jesus' Galilee or Paul's Corinth can come to life with media such as these. Again in this area, primary and secondary educators have worked harder to produce informative, illustrated texts (not to mention AV material on the Bible) than have those at higher levels; but all can take advantage.

4. Using and evaluating instructional media

Which presupposes that the teachers themselves are competent in the use of instructional media. **Certain communication competencies** can be listed. The teacher should know the basic types of communication media, their characteristics and capabilities. The teacher should know how to operate common media devices such as the OHP, tape recorder, slide projector, movie projector. The teacher should know the source of media materials which can be purchased for use in various settings.[14] Does this sound daunting to those of us raised on duplicators, chalk and talk, before the media explosion? We may need to take a few lessons from a colleague; but if in doubt, ask the students! Hopefully an amended curriculum in biblical institutes will include attention to educational technology, and so we shall all have these few skills. In addition, it would be desirable if the teacher could produce many kinds of simple materials (like slide-sound presentations) for use with small devices.

We should all, of course, also be expert these days in **evaluating the impact of the electronic media**. There is just the possibility that, having acquired these basic competencies, we rush into indiscriminate use of resources and media. We need constantly to be posing to ourselves questions such as the following:

Are my students capable of using the resources I recommend to them? are they readily available to them, or am I really just advertising my own erudition?

Are the instructional materials I am using suited to achieving the objectives of the lesson? do they help or hinder? are they distracting rather than reinforcing?

Are my visuals of a good standard? as the medium is the message, am I rather suggesting the subject is not worth careful, professional work on my part?

Is my reliance on audiovisual media excessive? have I disappeared as competent guide in the lesson? on the other hand, do I vary the 'talking head' sufficiently? do the students find me boring?[15]

---

[14] Haney and Ulmer, op.cit., 28. Cf A. Earathara, "Media at the service of the Word," Catechetics India 8 (1991 No.1) 23-30.
[15] Cf Romiszowski, Developing Auto-instructional Materials, 405-408.

Good will can be counted on in those who come to meet the Word in the text of Scripture, if not to the heroic extent of the eunuch endeavouring to wrestle with the text of Second Isaiah in a lurching chariot on the bumpy desert road from Jerusalem to Gaza. It is definitely false to the divine initiative of the Incarnation, however, if, relying on that good will, we do not take advantage of instructional resources and media available to assist that meeting, that *koinonia*. Teaching the Bible and learning the Bible can be considerably enriched by active acceptance of these aids to study. Sociologists like McLuhan remind us that that the Gutenberg age is over, that now the medium is the message, that our students could be receiving an inadequate message because the medium - ourselves as teachers - is inadequate to the task. We have in **the Incarnation the model** of a surprisingly imaginative medium,[16] adapted to our needs by a wonderful *synkatabasis*. Hopefully we can in some way follow this model in adapting our message imaginatively to today's students in the electric age.

Bibliography (print)

J. A. Fitzmyer, *An Introductory Bibliography for the Study of Scripture*, Rome: Pontifical Biblical Institute, 1990, 3rd ed.

J. B. Haney & E. J. Ulmer, *Educational Communications and Technology. An Introduction for Teachers*, Dubuque: Wm C. Brown, 1975, 2nd ed.

B. Hodge & D. Tripp, *Children and Television*, Cambridge: Polity Press, 1986

S. B. Marrow, *Basic Tools of Biblical Exegesis*, Rome: Pontifical Biblical Institute, 1978, 2nd ed.

---

[16] Cf J. McIntyre, *Faith, Theology and Imagination*, Edinburgh: The Handsell Press, 1987, 54.

A. J. Romiszowski, *Developing Auto-instructional Materials*, London: Kogan Page, 1986

_____ , *The Selection and Use of Instructional Media*, London: Kogan Page, 1988, 2nd ed.

D. Unwin & R. McAleese, *The Encyclopaedia of Educational Media Communications and Technology*, London: Macmillan, 1978

Audiovisual material

In the audiovisual area, by contrast with print media, there is no definitive catalogue or index (like *Religion Index One*), in keeping with the rapidly developing nature of these media.

For many decades in Europe, groups like the Salesians and the Society of St Paul produced filmstrips, photographic slide sets (with commentary on audio tape or print) and audio tapes to resource biblical education. In Britain and the United States similar audiovisual material was produced by

Our Sunday Visitor,
Noll Plaza,
Huntington IL 46750

Columbia Bible College,
PO Box 3122,
Columbia SC 29203

Jeffrey Norton Publishers,
On-the-Green,
Guilford CT

Alba House Communications,
PO Box 595,
Canfield OH 44406

Sound in Focus Ltd,
9 Sandy Lane,
Skelmersdale, Lanc,
WN8 8LA   UK

Cathedral Films Inc,
2921 W. Alameda Ave,
Burbank CA

Films on the Bible were also produced by these groups. The coming of television and the videotape recorder both simplified and made more sophisticated the use of these aids for an audience that developed higher expectations of AV media. Films, filmstrips and slides have been put in video form for convenience. Videos for use in biblical education are produced by firms such as

Veritas Video Productions,   Wesley Central Mission,
The Communications Centre,   210 Pitt St,
169 Booterstown Ave,   Sydney NSW 2000,
Blackrock, Co Dublin, Eire   Australia

Brown Roa Publishing Media,   Veritas Australia,
PO Box 539,   PO Box 566,
Dubuque IA 52004-0539   Fortitude Valley Q 4006

Southeast Pastoral Institute,   Antelope,
2900 SW 87th Ave,   3 Fitzroy Square,
Miami FL 33165   London W1P 5AH, UK

Needless to say, audiovisual materials vary greatly, not only in their level of production, but in the intention of the producers and the degree of fidelity to the biblical text and message. AV and graphic media have a particular fascination for fundamentalist groups.

(Reference to a computer database such as "AV On-line" would help locate particular AV items or a list of items under "Bible", "biblical education".)

Practical exercises for ministry

1. The deacon Philip was a godsend to the eunuch in his time of need of a minister of the Word. Could you honestly say that you are as informed and skilful a minister as your students (will) require as basic resource in this ministry? List what you have to offer them, and where deficiencies may lie. How will you remedy the latter?

2. You are taking part in a biblical studies course at tertiary level, and the lecturer has asked you to evaluate for the group the variety of Bible translations the students bring to the class. Decide on your criteria (in view of the level and purpose of this particular class), and make a judgement on the various modern translations (there being a number of revised ones on the market: *New RSV, New JB, New IV, New AB, Revised (N)EB)*. Only then compare your comments with those of a reviewer like Fitzmyer.

3. How interesting do you find your experience of the ministry of the Word to you (or do your students/parishioners find your exercise of it)? To what extent is this degree of satisfaction related to the use of instructional media? Could you suggest greater imaginativeness on the part of the minister?

4. You are to give a series of classes (at high school or tertiary level) on the Galilean ministry of Jesus. Sketch briefly the particular topics you will cover. Then, after visiting your local resource centre, list the instructional media available to assist with your presentations on these topics, and show how you will use them topic by topic.

Chapter Nine

Evaluating the teaching of Scripture

Outline

In the ministry of the Word too much is at stake in achieving that share in divine life offered in the Scriptures to allow us to neglect the responsibility of evaluating our ministerial efforts. We need to consider

- reasons for evaluating our teaching
- what elements of a course can be evaluated
- how conduct evaluation of our course
- what forms of student assessment are appropriate
- what limits there are to evaluation.

Our purpose in the exercise of the ministry of the Word is for people to participate in the benefits of the divine *koinonia* that the Scriptures represent. Without this ministry, that offer of life might not reach those beneficiaries. Hence the justification for the careful planning for ministry outlined in Chapter Five. There we also thought it useful to relate our efforts at precision in deciding on particular objectives in teaching and other ministries to eventual evaluation of our ministerial involvement; it helps to know first what we intended to achieve if we wish to gauge the success of our efforts. Why, though, concern ourselves with the outcome of our ministry? Is it **not mere curiosity** for us to want to estimate this success? Surely not: the necessity of biblical *koinonia* in the life of Christians is urgent reason enough for us to evaluate our efforts. The deacon Philip must have been encouraged in his apostolate by the eunuch's positive response to his guidance and his further request for baptism, though the text reminds us that, far from staying around to luxuriate in this ministerial achievement, "the Spirit of the Lord caught up Philip, and the eunuch saw him no more" (*Acts* 8.39).

Paul, on the other hand, might have asked himself if his preaching at Troas was achieving what he intended as at least one of his listeners "sank into a deep sleep as Paul talked still longer" and suffered a bad fall (*Acts* 20.7-9) - something of an object lesson for preachers and teachers. As well, there have always been those who have been tempted to estimate success in the ministry of the Word **in numerical terms**; Theodoret of Cyr in the fifth century in commenting on *Psalm* 2.8 sees a reference to words from the Song of Moses at *Deuteronomy* 32.43 (LXX):

> Thus he fulfilled the oracle of Moses, whose words were, "Rejoice, gentiles, with his people." Now, it is possible to discover an appropriate fulfilment for this prophecy, too: the number of Jews who came to faith were not only the twelve apostles but as well the seventy disciples, the hundred and twenty whom blessed Peter addressed in assembly, the five hundred to whom he appeared on one occasion after the resurrection according to the statement of the divinely inspired Paul, the three thousand and five thousand whom the chief of the apostles addressed in casting his net, and the many myriads of whom the mighty James exclaimed, "You see, brother, how many myriads of believers there are" - these, to be sure, and in addition to them those of the Jews throughout the world who have come to faith he declares a holy people, and through them he takes possession of all nations, thus fulfilling the prophecy in the words, "Rejoice, gentiles, with his people."[1]

1. Purpose of evaluation

Not surprisingly, educators have developed a more sophisticated rationale for evaluating educational effort. "Short of

---

[1] Commentary on the Psalms (*PG* 80, 880-81).

actually looking for course results, teachers should be receptive to the kinds of evidence that would indicate the effects a course has had. It is, after all, the anticipated results (i.e., goals) that justify a course. We owe it to both our students and ourselves to try to determine how sound our justification is."[2] Where the ministry of teaching the Scriptures is concerned and the overall goal biblical *koinonia*, the obligation is also to the Word, who is a third party in the relationship; **the Word was not spoken idly** and, as Isaiah reminded us, is not meant to be ineffectual, and that fact renders evaluation of our teaching even less optional. Much more is at stake if I prove to be merely beating the air, if I am but sounding brass or tinkling cymbal; it is not merely the behavioural modification that seems to be suggested by some literature on educational goals: life is at issue here. It would be good for me to recognise promptly the effect my ministry is having.

We do not have to look far for an overall justification of the ministry of the Word in general: it is as vital to all Christian growth as is other sacramental ministry, as we have seen *Dei Verbum* 21 reminding us. We may, however, need to justify the particular course on the Bible we are teaching by **balancing outcomes against intentions**, presuming we have planned carefully to meet the needs of a particular group or particular individuals (as we discussed in Chapter Five). Evaluation will consider those objectives we set ourselves, as well as any other outcomes and consequences of the course **foreseen and unforeseen**, and the whole process of education itself, involving teacher-student relationship, the focus of instruction, course organisation, physical situation, student attitudes to the course, unexpected developments. Reviewing all these factors will help us do more than justify (or, possibly, question) this particular course (*summative evaluation*); it will enable us to decide which aspects of the course should be modified or improved (*formative evaluation*), it will allow us (if this is appropriate) to *assess*

---

[2] G. J. Posner, A. N. Rudnitsky, *Course Design. A Guide to Curriculum Development for Teachers*, 167.

students' response or even diagnose obstacles to an individual's response, it may shed light on an overall program or institutional curriculum.[3] These are the **various purposes served by evaluation** of courses, sessions, group work, independent study of the Scriptures. It is not primarily designed to show up my strengths or weaknesses as a teacher, though both Philip and Paul (not to mention Father Rufus) could have learnt much about this from the response of their listeners on those celebrated occasions.

2. What to evaluate

To see more clearly the scope and process of evaluation in the ministry of the Word, let us return to the teaching situation taken as example in Chapter Five. We were invited to work in a parish situation with a group of Catholic parents anxious to "learn (more) about the Bible". We saw from the first session that none had any (recent) acquaintance with the Scriptures beyond the Gospels and were not accustomed to handling a Bible. So we set ourselves as our modest objectives certain basic skills and understandings about the Bible generally. It is now the end of the first ten sessions that we decided on as sufficient for one year, and we would like to *evaluate* **progress** with a view to making adjustment (if the level has been too high, for instance, or the pace too slow) for next year, and to detecting any major blockages in an individual's approach (perhaps a reading difficulty, a certain racial background, a fundamentalist predisposition); *assessment* **of achievement** in terms of grades for reporting is not appropriate with this well-motivated, non-competitive group of parents.

We begin at the basic level of skills ('psychomotor-perceptual skills'), with a speed test, nominating a dozen verses throughout the Bible and asking the group to find the speaker in each verse without reference to Table of Contents, page tabs, or any other aid; they are simply to rely on their ability to find their way around

---

[3] Cf N. E. Gronlund, *Measurement and Evaluation in Teaching*, 11.

that pesky book. We proceed to test cognitive understanding and skills by nominating a dozen books of the Old Testament, and asking them to assign these to the main divisions of the Hebrew Bible as outlined during the course. Affective understanding and skills come into play when we distribute a copy of chapter 12 of *Ecclesiastes*, not studied in class, and ask the group to write down their views on the subject matter and their response to the sentiments of this writer on the onset of old age.

We learn much from this part of the evaluation procedure. All who have attended regularly and have brought their Bibles with them have little difficulty completing the speed test in the space of seven or eight minutes; irregular attenders are lost. The same is true of the exercise on divisions of the Old Testament. But in the 'unseen', even some of the regular attenders have problems because they either don't read easily or can't recognise pathos where it occurs. We feel we can next time proceed to look more closely at the text (selected portions) of books within these biblical divisions - some *Exodus* from the Torah, from the Former Prophets the story of Solomon's accession from both *1 Kings* and *1 Chronicles* (for comparative purposes), the book of *Jonah*, some proverbs and psalms - touching on some questions of authorship, composition, biblical truth and inspiration that arise from these books. But it is also clear we are going to have to take things more slowly with those who cannot read freely and those who are not used to responding to literature.

There is another part of evaluation with our group of beginners, however, beyond the goal-based estimation outlined above testing the objectives we set ourselves initially. **The whole process of teaching** should come under scrutiny if we are to assess the effectiveness of our ministry of the Word and make decisions for improving the usefulness of our sessions; we are interested, remember, in teaching not simply as transmission of information but also as transaction, process, and even as transformation of attitude and living. There may be a number of **side effects** of our course we did not envisage. We may, for instance, detect an inbred fundamentalist streak in some students, reacting negatively to our critical study of the text. Others may find our treatment too pedestrian, not catering sufficiently for the spiritual development of the listeners. These effects we can discover in **various ways** (and at various times: formative evaluation should be occurring from the outset): chatting with students individually throughout the course, staging a formal evaluation session that is both open-ended and directed to some general quesions, distributing a questionnaire of the same character.

Responses may touch on a number of **matters, foreseen and unforeseen.** One may deal with the degree of correspondence between what the members expected to meet in class work and what actually happened, what they expected to gain and what they felt they did gain; they could be alternately satisfied, disappointed, thrilled, overwhelmed, shocked, bored. Father Rufus's students did not respond as he expected, and it would have been in the interests of everyone for him to evaluate this response. A helpful question in exercises like this is what did students find most helpful and what least helpful. Another matter might be relationships between group and teacher, or with one another: was there interaction enough? This relates also to the model of adult learning followed: was there opportunity to share, was it instead 'jug-to-mug' teaching, was there any sense of search and discovery? Was the teacher sympathetic enough to individual differences, to the slow learners, to those in the group who come from other cultural or religious backgrounds? There may be organisational matters, like timing of sessions, seating arrangements, amenities. Mention might also be made of the effect on the group meetings of unexpected events, like illness, interruption, unavoidable absence of the lecturer.

Had we been working instead with a well-grounded class at tertiary level on, say, Old Testament theology or exegesis, evaluation would consider a wider range of objectives and reach also to **assessment of their performance** with a view to grading them and reporting these grades. We would test their memory, comprehension and commitment to material from *Isaiah* 1-39 (for instance) by their ability to verbalise, define, recognise, identify, describe, compare, justify, defend, argue[4] - indicators of growth in understanding. For instance, we could require them to establish a case for the independence of this prophet from his sixth century namesakes by detailing his distinctive themes and accents, thus arguing for an eighth century Sitz im Leben.

Their **affective understanding** of this semester's biblical material would emerge from the appreciation and empathy they show with, say, the women in those 'texts of terror' Phyllis Trible discusses.[5] We might have them examine in close detail the story of the Levite's concubine in *Judges* 19 for the author's awareness of a woman's sensibility, hoping they may light upon such pathetic details as the last few words of verse 27. We could assess as well the class's **cognitive skills** in planning, devising and describing where difficulty and transfer are involved, perhaps by bringing canonical considerations to bear on non-canonical material like Ethiopian *Enoch* or *The Testaments of the Twelve Patriarchs*.

As to the **types of testing** more appropriate, it would seem essay type assignments would suit biblical material at this tertiary level better than objective tests, though oral examination would also allow estimation of these understandings to be made. We could alternatively ask students to take responsibility for a chapter of our text and lead discussion of it in class; they might prepare an annotated bibliography of the topic being studied, or review articles on it. Occasionally assessment could take a practical bent by requiring students to suggest ways of bringing the biblical message to a particular audience. In deciding on the form of assessment, we would need to take into account, as well as the

---

[4] Cf Posner and Rudnitsky, *Course Design*, 160-66.
[5] *Texts of Terror: Literary-Feminist Readings of Biblical Narratives*, Philadelphia: Fortress, 1984.

kind of information we are looking for and the level of the group, also the time needed for the test, the size of the group, and the facilities available. Casual and formal evaluation procedures could gauge the degree of student satisfaction with our course.

3. Limits to evaluation

Gathering information on all these matters should help us in our summative evaluation of the course's overall success, and in formative evaluation that addresses the possibility of adjustment. Educators warn against raising **unrealistic expectations** with the procedure or questionnaire employed, and against asking the students to rate our performance as a teacher - a question that is probably too general to be helpful by comparison with more reliable indicators and that can discourage some teachers from attempting any evaluation at all. **Students' privacy** at all levels should also be respected: concerned though we are to promote that meeting between the Word and the believer through the Scriptures, it is not for us to pry or to endeavour to estimate the degree of faith response of these readers of the Word. The text of *Acts* is clear on the distance Philip keeps from his willing pupil's joyful encounter with that Word; the movement from faith to baptism comes solely from the delighted discoverer. This sensitive matter has been given much attention in the case of assessment in religious education of school pupils and reporting of that assessment.[6] This is not to deny that some contexts and forms of ministry of the Word can prove to be not only faith building but also faith sharing situations: our small group of Christian parents will almost certainly become a locus for sharing faith experiences in the course of our sessions as we learn to trust one another better. But the principle of privacy remains valid in this consideration of evaluating our teaching of Scripture.

---

[6] M. Macdonald, "Assessment of affective objectives in religious education," *Word in Life* 38 (1990 February) 22-26.

There are **other limits and limitations** to evaluation of educational processes. Time itself, valuable though the exercise is, is not unlimited; evaluation should not dominate the teaching being evaluated. Reliability is another factor; it is not unusual for questions to be framed and responses to be given in such a way that they are biased and do not allow the true situation to emerge. Students can become inured to frank, thoughtful participation in evaluation procedures by the very frequency of the exercise. These limitations, however, do not obscure the value and need for taking stock of our ministry.

For the Fathers, teaching is the "art of arts and science of sciences", presumably because it is concerned with the total development of people. In a particular way does introduction to the Word of God contribute to this rounded development - a comprehensive growth that is done scant justice in some educational literature that speaks only of behavioural modification that can be mechanically monitored by limited evaluation procedures. The ministry of the Word in its various forms is aimed **as much at spiritual development as at measurable outcomes**. What we are in fact hoping to achieve is, ultimately, that growth in faith, hope and love that Augustine set himself as a goal in his teaching.

> Whatever you say, say it in such a way that on hearing it your listeners may come to believe, by believing may come to hope, and by hoping may come to love.[7]

No wonder Vatican II begins its Constitution on the Word with these sentiments. The model of the biblically literate person was also spelled out in the New Testament by the author of the Pastorals; it is interesting that evaluation of the encounter between the Christian reader and the Scriptures was left by him to life indicators:

---

[7] *De Catechizandis Rudibus* 4, 8 (PL 40, 316).

For your part, hold fast to what you have learnt and have come
to believe, conscious of whom you learnt it from, and how since
childhood you have known the sacred writings. They have the
power to give you the sense of direction that leads to salvation
through faith in Christ Jesus. All Scripture, inspired as it is, is
valuable for instructing, for reproving, for correcting, for
guidance in good living, so that the person who is God's is now
ready for anything, equipped for every good work.[8]

Bibliography

N. E. Gronlund, *Measurement and Evaluation in Teaching*, New York:
Macmillan, 1985, 2nd ed.

B. S. Bloom, G. F. Madaus, J. T. Hastings, *Evaluation to Improve
Learning*, New York: McGraw-Hill, 1981

L. Brady, *Curriculum Development*, Sydney: Prentice-Hall, 1990, 3rd ed.

L. J. Cronbach, *Essentials of Psychological Testing*, New York: Harper and
Row, 1984, 4th ed.

W. A. Mehrens, I. J. Lehmann, *Measurement and Evaluation in
Education and Psychology*, New York: Holt, Rinehart & Winston, 1984

W. J. Popham, *Modern Educational Measurement*, Englewood Cliffs:
Prentice-Hall, 1981

G. J. Posner, A. N. Rudnitsky, *Course Design. A Guide to Curriculum
Development for Teachers*, New York-London: Longman, 1982, 2nd ed.

M. Print, *Curriculum Development and Design*, Sydney: Allen & Unwin,
1988

D. Rowntree, *Assessing Students: How Shall We Know Them*, London:
Harper and Row, 1977

---

[8] *2 Tm* 3.14-17.

Practical exercises for ministry

1. Are you in the habit of evaluating your efforts in the ministry of the Word? What criteria do you apply to gauge your success? Construct an evaluation sheet that would suit your most recent exercise of that ministry.

2. You are at the stage of assessing student achievement in the series of lessons you gave on the Galilean ministry of Jesus (Exercise 4 of the previous chapter) with a view to reporting. Discuss what is involved in your choice of a suitable test, and develop the test.

3. Father Rufus, we saw, found his course on *Revelation* did not go well; students did not respond as planned. Suggest to him how, instead of his simply being disappointed, a proper formative evaluation procedure could have helped him and the students.

4. How could the principles of evaluation outlined in this chapter help a preacher of the Word (as, for example, your own pastor) evaluate his ministry?

Conclusion

Conclusion

Formation for ministry

The conclusion arising from these pages devoted to a study of the ministry of the Word in general and the particular ministry of teaching the Word is identical with the conviction that prompted the writing: **the urgent need for ministerial preparation**. Those intending to minister the Word to others, to introduce them to that share in divine life, *koinonia*, that the Scriptures represent, must know not simply the Word but as well the principles and practice of ministry. The responsibility for ensuring this adequate formation of future ministers lies in particular with **biblical institutes** that have been entrusted with biblical education. This text has been prepared to highlight the need, pinpoint certain deficiencies in ministerial formation in some cases, and outline the general and particular principles of curriculum change.

Because the answer lies to a large extent in the **curriculum** of those institutions charged with ministerial formation. A text can be merely a stimulus and guide. As was stated above, no one ever learned to be an effective teacher merely through reading a book; "the art of arts and science of sciences" is not acquired as simply as that. None of the caring professions in today's world would be satisfied with a formation that did not directly address **the practical preparation of aspirants** in addition to provision of a theoretical base for professional involvement. Admittedly, in the case of the ministry of the Word, the very acquaintance with that Word is an enriching, even vivifying, experience. But as the Word incarnate in the person of Jesus did not succeed, and has not since in various times and cultures succeeded, in winning all to himself automatically by his mere coming, so the ministry of that Word today also has a range of challenges and problems to take account of in ensuring an efficacious meeting of Word and listener. "Faith comes through hearing" may be true of our time as of Paul's; in this electric age with its multimedia communication, however, the minister has to work harder to make sure attention is secured and the message heard.

1. Challenges and opportunities

If the **challenges** today for the minister of the Word are greater, the **advantages and resources** for ministry are more abundant. We have available an accumulated lore to do with the way people learn and can be effectively taught, we have been reminded to respect the influence of their culture on teaching and learning, we can profit from experiments with forms and contexts of ministry, new approaches and programs. Our times have developed a wide range of instructional media to enrich the ministry of the Word.

Hence, there is no excuse for biblical institutes failing to devise **an adequate curriculum for rounded preparation of ministers**, especially with contemporary encouragement from the magisterium in this direction. A sample program is offered in this volume, but it is generic only, touching on issues that require consideration everywhere. Institutions in particular situations meeting particular needs will have to incorporate these issues in a curriculum of their own devising, beginning (as always in an exercise of curriculum development) with the needs and situation of the intended beneficiaries: worshippers in the pews of affluent churches, students in large or small classrooms and lecture halls, adult groups in conditions of deprivation and ignorance, children of various ages, prayer groups, retreatants.

2. Towards an adequate curriculum

Curriculum adjustment can be a painful exercise; it is a question of setting or redistributing priorities, and that calls for honesty, detachment and even courage. In an institution that has been accustomed to think of biblical education in academic terms only and neglect the ministerial involvement of its students (with the unfortunate but inevitable effects we depicted in our imaginary Father Rufus, typical product of such formation), rethinking and reconstruction are called for. The **institutional profile** will need to be rethought to allow inclusion of formal treatment of theoretical and practical aspects of the ministry of the Word beyond the usual textual and contextual studies of the Bible. **Personnel** may need to be called on for advice or teaching. Other institutional **resources**, such as library holdings and audiovisual equipment, may need to be supplemented. Even **physical arrangements** at the institution, such as lecture and tutorial rooms, may require alteration if provision is to be made for modelling of desirable ministerial situations, such as small group work, or for use of instructional media.

This is to suggest that preparation for ministry depends not only on institutional curriculum but on **practical initiation** as well (as in those other caring professions referred to). Paul's Damascus experience may have given him sufficient impulse to conduct an extraordinary ministry for a couple of decades; but (as we have hinted in Chapter Nine) a more typical, even mundane, preparation could have alerted him to the dangers of allowing listeners to drop off during excessively long sermons, and could perhaps also have improved a style of speaking and deportment apparently not above reproach. Teacher education continues to rest on the truth that there is no substitute for experience, and that initiation into that instructive experience can be prepared for, monitored and evaluated with a view to improved participation of the neophyte and less frustrating process for the pupils/recipients. There is arguably no situation where good will and initiative cannot set up such **learning experiences** for would-be ministers; only institutional inertia stands in the way, perhaps due to ignorance of magisterial and educational advances touched on in this text.

Good will, surely, is fundamental in this reconstruction of institutional curriculum; unless staff not simply accept but actively support these modifications for rounded ministerial preparation of aspirants, they will wither under the influence of lack of esteem, with inevitable effects on the aspirants' own priorities. Of course, modelling of good ministry by the professors of the institution would be a bonus, but tertiary students learn to make allowances; so formal attention to ministry in the curriculum should not provoke feelings of inadequacy in the staff, even if at some stage they might welcome the opportunity for their own ministry to undergo renewal.

3. Updating ministers in service

After all, serving ministers of the Word, like professionals the world over, even if graduates of less enlightened times, can profit from **continuing education opportunities**, variously called in-service or post-service (as distinct from pre-service, undergraduate). Father Rufus, for instance, graduate of an institute with a curriculum not attending to the students' ministerial involvement, could profitably have availed himself of such opportunities on discovering his teaching was not having the results intended. Perhaps attendance at a workshop on evaluation procedures (or even reading a text like this) would have allowed him to diagnose the shortcomings of his courses from his own and the students' point of view. He could perhaps recognise the need for planning to meet *these* students' needs in particular and relate to their stage of development. Further inservice assistance would help him adopt a model of learning suited to these young adults, and take advantage of available resources and today's media in his teaching. Practitioners of other professions everywhere take pains to update themselves, and assistance is available also to ministers of the Word.

What is said here, and what is contained by way of principle in this whole text, is applicable not simply to biblical education but to **the ministry of the Word in the widest sense**, wherever preparation for the communication of the Good News is involved. It is therefore not solely biblical institutes that need to construct a curriculum that attends to principles of ministry, but also theological faculties, moral academies, seminaries, religious education institutions generally. It could in fact be claimed that Catholic people have found speakers to the biblical text less mystifying than preachers on general theological themes. As has been observed above, those tertiary institutions preparing teachers of the young have generally provided for theoretical and practical preparation for communication of Christian doctrine; any deficiencies in their curriculum, at least in western Catholic communities, lie rather with recognition of the importance of the Bible, and this deficiency is in process of correction since Vatican II. So understanding of ministry and its implications should be a core element of curriculum in all theological institutions; Father Rufus could have been equally ineffectual in other areas of pastoral care without proper preparation.

4. The spirituality of the minister

A final word of qualification. It would be a misreading of this text to conclude that effective ministry of the Word depends on techniques and gadgetry. Yes, the Incarnation suggests that in communicating the Word we take advantage of all that inventiveness, scholarship and the passage of time have provided for assisting biblical *koinonia*, for breaking the bread of the Word. But Augustine reminded us, and *Dei Verbum* repeats the reminder, that it is **growth in faith** that is the desired outcome of this ministry, and we know that faith comes from faith; even the learning theorists have highlighted the place of our own beliefs in the knowledge of a subject that enthuses the learner.

The author of the Pastoral Epistles, we saw, himself convinced of the value of Christian praxis and the ordering of the Scriptures to that end, nevertheless insisted on **the minister's own spirituality**, "the sense of direction that leads to salvation through faith in Christ Jesus;" for him it was only "the person who is God's" who with the instruction of Scripture "is now ready for anything, equipped for every good work" (2 *Tm* 3.15-17). Uninspired use of technological wizardry in the ministry of the Word would, of course, be the modern equivalent of sounding brass and tinkling cymbal. What is required is that that great minister Chrysostom's ideal for the Word would become a reality: "The reading of the Scriptures is an opening of the heavens." We must do what we can to ensure that when our people meet the Word, the heavens do open. Sufficient reason for conscientious, informed ministry.

Appendix One

A program for ministerial formation

The need for institutes preparing people for the ministry of the Word, and especially teaching the Scriptures, to address the requirements of ministerial involvement in their curriculum has been highlighted in this text. What is offered here of a generic kind is a program that could be included *mutatis mutandis* in an institute's curriculum, while allowing that some of the considerations are cross-curriculum as well and not confined to one slot in the institute's timetable: knowledge of learning theories, for instance, benefits professors and students in all discipline areas.

Taking a leaf out of our own book, we follow the process of program design outlined in Chapter Five, "Planning for a ministry of the Word".

Stage 1

In terms of **ministerial priorities** we are in no doubt of the urgency of this treatment for the proper formation of our would-be ministers of the Word.

Our **overall educational goals** are set by Scripture itself, that in terms of the ministry of the Word "the person who is God's is now equipped for anything, equipped for every good work" (2 *Tm* 3.17), able to promote a fruitful meeting between Word and listener.

The **principles of teaching and learning** we will follow are those that have been found successful in bringing a group of young adults of this size to understand and appropriate the general principles of ministry, and put them into practice in a supervised practicum.

The needs of this group, their stage of development and cultural diversity, their likely form of ministerial involvement all dictate the way the course will be planned and implemented. (In this case we are dealing with a group of future teachers of the Bible.) The student group can help us arrive at precision in this **situational analysis**.

Stage 2

Our intended outcome in this part of the course is that students will obtain a sound **theoretical base** for their ministry of teaching through presentation of general and particular principles. **Practical application** of principle will occur in working through exercises and being involved in practicum situations.

The following are the **content areas** to be presented:

I Word and ministry

- the nature of the scriptural Word
- an understanding of revelation as *koinonia*
- the need for the Word to be communicated
- the nature of ministry in general
- Church teaching on the ministry of the Word

II Readiness for the Word

- importance of considering the condition of the recipient
- relevant findings of developmental sciences
- assistance from theories about (adult) learning
- fidelity to needs and capacities as well as to the Word

III Respecting cultural differences

- cultural conditioning of the Word
- cultural conditioning of the listener
- the need for inculturating the biblical message
- teaching and learning in various cultures

IV Forms and contexts of the ministry of the Word

- forms of ministry
- traditional contexts of ministry
- effect of developments in society and technology
- different approaches in traditional forms of ministry

V Planning for ministry

- the purpose of the Word
- a rationale for ministry
- differentiating between experiences and learning outcomes
- planning a ministerial task
- stages of planning

VI The ministry of teaching the Scriptures

- ministerial principles in teaching
- equipping the teacher
- the teacher as communicator

VII What to teach

- communicating the teacher's own scholarship
- study of the text of Scripture
- a wider viewpoint through hermeneutical principles
- appealing to feeling as well as reason
- what to teach adults
- what to teach children

VIII How to teach the Bible

   - examples from Scripture
   - different learning models
   - settings, contexts, approaches, programs
   - how to teach adults
   - how to teach children

IX Teaching resources and instructional media

   - the biblical text as resource
   - contextual resources
   - available instructional media
   - matching media to modes of instruction
   - knowing how to use instructional media
   - evaluating the use of resources and media

X Evaluating the teaching of Scripture

   - reasons for evaluating our teaching
   - what evaluation achieves
   - what can be evaluated and assessed
   - limits and limitations of evaluation

The division of material suggests **planning** for ten sessions with the group. The style of teaching, the approach, the setting will depend on the number and maturity of the group. We need to consider the availability of textual and audiovisual resources and media of instruction.

Stage 3

With these adults we arrange for sessions marked by intimacy and participation as far as possible as opposed to impassive attention to unbroken lecturing. After each item of the day's topic we invite questions and general student exchange. **Each session** includes practical exercises for ministry completed at the time or in study time between sessions; these can be assessed and returned to students to help lecturer and students keep an account of progress. The smallness of the group and style of teaching also allow for evaluative comments from individuals.

Towards the latter part of the course students begin their **practicum** experiences with groups of people (adults and children) in nearby parishes, schools or other settings under the supervision of institute staff. (These experiences also call for careful planning and evaluation.)

Stage 4

In addition to the cumulative assessment of student work and evaluative comments throughout the course, there is need at the conclusion to **address the success of the program** in terms of expected outcomes, side effects, teacher-student relationship, course organisation, the physical situation, etc. Formal evaluative instruments, like examination and questionnaire, may be employed as well as less formal interchange made possible by the relatively unstructured situation. The institution may require reporting of student results, and may wish to consider the advisability of repeating the program in future. We ourselves utilise the information thus gathered to adjust course structure.

Appendix Two

Rite of Christian Initiation of Adults: an occasion for ministry of the Word

A form of the ministry of the Word that flourished in the early Church, later to wane, has been revived with the restoration of the adult catechumenate following Vatican II. There is now provision for an initiation of adults into the community which "may be sanctified by sacred rites to be celebrated at successive intervals of time" (Constitution on the Sacred Liturgy 64). This graduated introduction of the candidate for initiation may extend from precatechumenate to postbaptismal catechesis, or mystagogy; the most significant stage is that of catechumenate.

Of relevance to the ministry of the Word is the role of Scripture in this initiation process; at every stage the candidates are introduced to, even immersed in, the Scriptures, particularly the Gospels. The rite takes its cue from the Council again:

> Sacred Scripture is of paramount importance in the celebration of the liturgy. For it is from Scripture that lessons are read and explained in the homily, and psalms are sung; the prayers, collects, and liturgical songs are scriptural in their inspiration, and it is from Scripture that actions and signs derive their meaning. Thus, if the restoration, progress and adaptation of the sacred liturgy are to be achieved, it is necessary to promote that warm and living love for Scripture to which the venerable tradition of both Eastern and Western rites give testimony (24).

The theology of baptism in the revised Roman Ritual is likewise appropriately scriptural (cf *The Rites of the Catholic Church*, 1A, New York: Pueblo Publishing Co, 1988, 3-5).

The success of this graduated process of initiation depends on the availability of competent and imaginative ministers to ensure that the intention of the rite is respected, namely, that "celebrations of the Word of God are foremost" among the various components. Each stage of initiation includes a liturgy of the Word. Within that liturgy at the Rite of Acceptance into the order of catechumens, a Bible is presented to each catechumen after the homily. The bishop has the responsibility of ensuring there are ministers capable of "giving the candidates a suitable explanation of the Gospel"; these may be "priests and deacons, catechists and other laypersons". They are to be capable of planning suitable celebrations of the Word on some occasions, at other times to follow readings prescribed in the Lectionary.

The responsibility of these ministers of the Word in the catechumenate is no light one; they are expected to ensure "the catechumens are properly initiated into the mysteries of salvation and the practice of an evangelical way of life." After initiation there follows the period of postbaptismal catechesis, "a time for the community and the neophyte together to grow in deepening their grasp of the paschal mystery and in making it part of their lives through meditation on the Gospel, sharing in the eucharist, and doing the works of charity." To this end the Ritual rightly speaks of "celebrations of the Word", not a mere service of readings. More is required of the minister than an ability to mouth words if the neophytes are to enter joyfully into that *koinonia* often spoken of in this text. In the period when this form of ministry flourished in the Church, Chrysostom could claim, "Here I am, lighting the fire of Scripture, and the lamp of its teaching is enkindled on my lips." The RCIA will depend for its success on such committed ministers of the Word; for these candidates, not yet able to approach the table of the body of the Lord, the bread of life must be taken from the table of the Word and expertly broken for their nourishment.

Appendix Three

The Bible (study) group:
a form of ministry of the Word

Earlier in this book, in Chapter Seven on appropriate contexts and settings for the ministry of teaching the Scriptures, we heard from people experienced in bringing adults into touch with the Bible in small groups. Experience with such groups is wide and generally favourable, though there are pitfalls to be avoided; stratagems have been developed over time and materials produced. We might consider here more formally this form of ministry of the Word, having an eye to the practitioners quoted in that Chapter Seven.

Bible groups vary in their precise objectives, though their overall aim - like that of the ministry of the Word in general - is to bring people to share in the *koinonia*, the offer of life, that a generous God gives us in the Scriptures. The groups are usually composed of adults, including those unfamiliar with the Bible. They may meet on a regular basis (weekly or fortnightly) over an indefinite period, or for a limited period, for a precise purpose, following a particular program (for instance, in preparation for the Seventh Assembly of the World Council of Churches in Canberra, Australia, in February 1991, when Christians around the world at the previous Pentecost began a program of six Bible sessions for which a helpful booklet was available with the Assembly's theme as title, *Come, Holy Spirit, Renew the Whole Creation* [Geneva: WCC]).

Not all Bible groups are Bible study groups, and in fact many people would be discouraged from this form of *koinonia* if it was presented as an intellectual exercise. Some groups meet **simply to respond to the Word of God** in the biblical text (perhaps of the approaching Sunday liturgy), which they read, ponder on, respond to, pray about, apply to their lives. The presence in the group of some members with a deeper biblical culture would help provide guidance when sought and avoid certain errors, but would be seen as bonus, not prerequisite or incubus. The only text is the Bible, or even simply liturgical readings in a Sunday missal.

Such groups have in common with study groups at least a **community character**; we saw William Riley relating this to the community origins of the biblical text. The theological appropriateness of the community setting has recently been emphasised by the International Council for Catechesis in its instruction, *Adult Catechesis in the Christian Community. Some Principles and Guidelines* (Rome: Libreria Editrice Vaticana, 1990):

> The communitarian dimension of the contents of faith will be thoroughly developed. In this way, adults will come to know and experience the "mystery of the Church", which is incarnate in a particular community and history and which is characterised by particular needs, initiatives and pace of life. Catechesis will help adults see how they can fit in and participate in the life of the Church (53).

Participants in such Bible sharing groups have in fact admitted that the experience has, perhaps for the first time, given them a sense of Church, as the Instruction suggests is one likely outcome.

Otherwise, **the Bible study group** is distinguished by its educational objectives, which participants are aware of, as distinct from formational and social objectives (Riley's distinction in his *The Bible Study Group. An Owner's Manual*, Notre Dame: Ave Maria Press, 1985). Writers such as Riley and Jerome Kodell (*The Catholic Bible Study Handbook*, Ann Arbor: Servant Books, 1985) are at pains to point out the implications of this different objective: the need and role of an informed group leader, structural considerations like situation, frequency, time, length, availability of resources, use of instructional media.

For these Bible study groups **programs** have been devised to promote the purposes of learning (cf Kodell, *op.cit.*, 212-13) and put less burden on the creativity of the leader. One such program that has been widely used and favourably received in parishes in the United States is that developed in the diocese of Little Rock, Arkansas, though adapted from a Protestant program used worldwide, Bible Study Fellowship. Its origins explain its concentration on the biblical text (at least of the New Testament), beginning with *Acts* (as resembling parish life) and moving finally to *Revelation*. Materials include booklets, tapes, videos; leaders are trained, experts are not required. Groups meet weekly for a limited time, having already been set written study tasks, for which a cheap commentary is available. The evening meetings include prayer, discussion and input from lecturer or tape.

The ABIL program referred to in Chapters Six and Seven is also unashamedly study-oriented. It is distinctive in being soundly based on modern educational principles - hence its emphasis on small-group interdependent learning - and in its formal adoption of contemporary biblical scholarship. It does not let the adult learners off easily with attention only to the New Testament or with a thematic approach; the course begins with the Old Testament, book by book. Group leaders are thoroughly trained, and study guides available. Based in the US, ABIL has trained teams for work in Canada, New Zealand and Australia.

The popularity of Little Rock and ABIL programs demonstrates the hunger for the Word in the (Catholic) faithful.

Abbreviations

AAS	*Acta Apostolicae Sedis*
ABIL	adult biblical interdependent learning
ASS	*Acta Sancta Sedis*
A V	audiovisual
A V	*Authorised Version* (of the Bible)
DAS	*Divino Afflante Spiritu*
DV	*Dei Verbum*
ET	English translation
OHP	overhead projector
PACE	*Professional Approaches for Christian Educators*
PG	*Patrologia Graeca*
PL	*Patrologia Latina*
RCIA	Rite of Christian Initiation of Adults
RE	religious education
TEV	*Today's English Version* (of the Bible)
TF	French translation
VTR	videotape recorder

General Index

abracadabra, 14
ABIL, 109,127,174
Abraham, 48,50
Absalom, 124
Ad Gentes, 41
African, 45,50
Alexandria, 51
andragogy, 117,123
anointing, 50
anthropology, 44,48
Antioch, 16,28,51,52,64
apocalyptic, 52,93,100
Aramaic, 42
archeology, 3,19,130,133,140
Areopagus, 52
artists, 44,58,126
audiovisual, 45,63,126,135-44
assessment, 149-56,168
Asia, 94
Australia, 52,93
authorship, 34,51,82,83,132,150

Babylon, 7
Barnabas, 77
Beatitudes, 125
Bethlehem, 27
Bible groups, 120-22,172-74
Bible societies, 17,50,59,130
Biblicum, i,19
Black preaching, 66
blessing, 50
Britain, 143

Canaan, 42
Canada, 174
canon, 4,152
catalogue, 143
Catechesi Tradendae, 20,36,63
catechesis, 7,20,25,35,36,47,48,54,55-67,96,170

catechumen, 170-71
Catholic Biblical Federation, 17,59
Central Africa, 50
China, 47
Christifideles Laici, 65
computers, 44,126,136-37,144
Confraternity of Christian Doctrine, 59,81
considerateness,10,22,23,28,45,60,89,126
Constantinople, 16
Constitution on the Sacred Liturgy, 69,170
Cornelius, 34
covenant, 101,104
criticism, 3,100,104,151
culture, 41-54,89,131,167
curriculum, *passim*
cursing, 50

Damascus, 161
data banks, 44
database, 135,136,144
David, 77
Decree on Priestly Formation, 73
Dei Verbum, passim
demythologise, 43
Denmark, 29
developmentalists, 29-34,37,40,89,110,111,166
Divino Afflante Spiritu, 4,11,20,57,59,73
drama, 67,124,125

East, 16,65,78,123,170
ecclesiology, 2
Egypt, 42,133
Elijah, 42
Elisha, 42
Emmaus, 80,124

Index of biblical citations

Index of authors

Finito di stampare il 28 giugno 1991
Tipografia Poliglotta della Pontificia Università Gregoriana
Piazza della Pilotta, 4 – 00187 Roma